Zulu Names, Polygyny and Gender Politics
in Traditional Societies

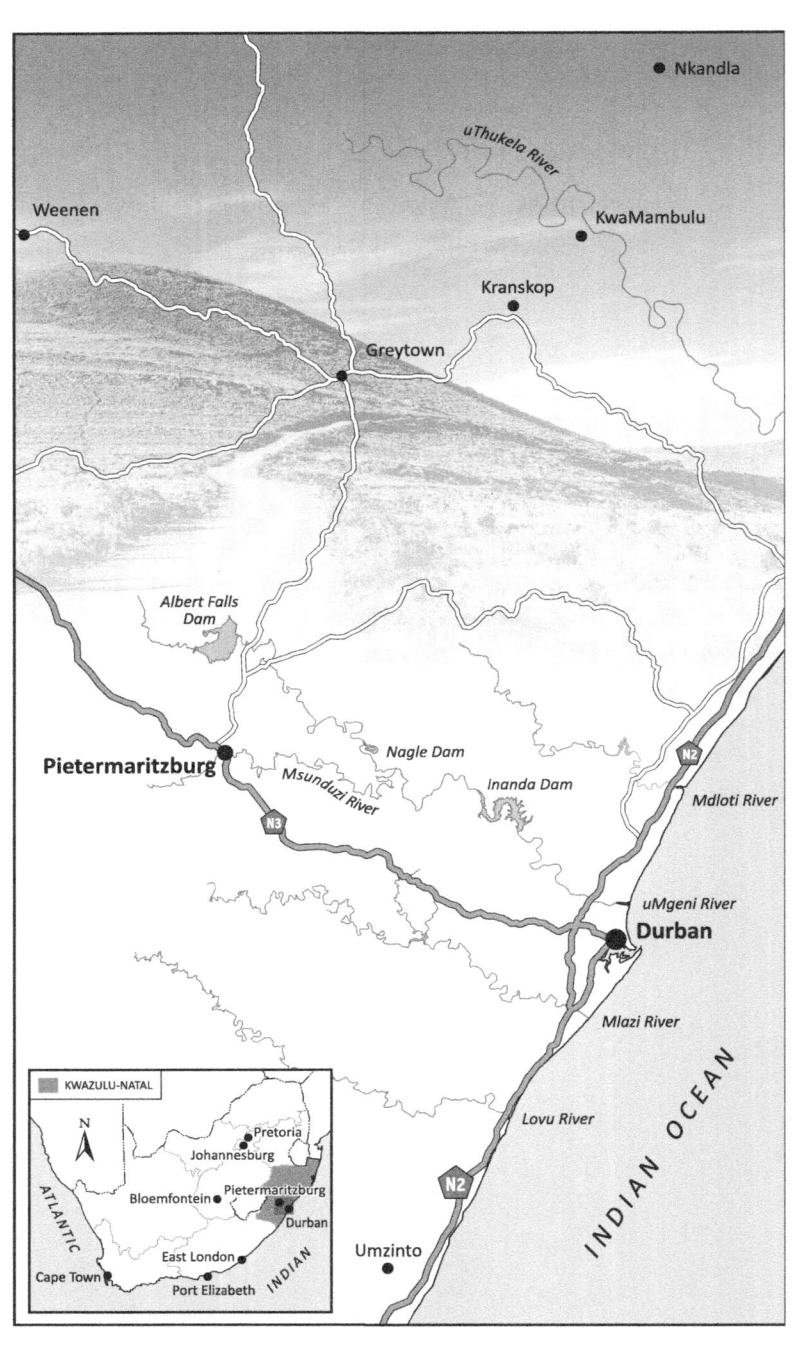

Zulu Names, Polygyny and Gender Politics in Traditional Societies

Evangeline Bonisiwe Zungu

UNIVERSITY OF KwaZulu-Natal Press

Published in 2021 by University of KwaZulu-Natal Press
Private Bag X01
Scottsville, 3201
Pietermaritzburg
South Africa
Email: books@ukzn.ac.za
Website: www.ukznpress.co.za

© 2021 Evangeline Bonisiwe Zungu

All rights reserved. No part of this publication may be reproduced or transmitted in any form or by electrical or mechanical means, including information storage and retrieval systems, without prior permission in writing from the publishers.

ISBN: 978 1 86914 470 8
e-ISBN: 978 1 86914 471 5

Project manager: Sally Hines
Editor: Alison Lockhart
Layout: Patricia Comrie
Proofreader: Cathy Munro
Indexer: Christopher Merrett
Cover design: Marise Bauer, M Design
Cover photograph: Paul Weinberg / Africa Media Online

The financial assistance of the National Institute of Humanities and Social Sciences (NIHSS) towards this publication is hereby acknowledged. Opinions expressed and conclusions arrived at are those of the author and are not necessarily to be attributed to the NIHSS.

Printed and bound in South Africa by Creda Communications

I dedicate this book to my daughter, Thokola Zungu.
Nyama kayishi isha ngabaphephezeli! Geda kaGwabini!

Contents

Acknowledgements	ix
Introduction	1
1 The Way of Life in KwaMambulu	27
2 Polygyny, Gender and Power in Traditional Societies	44
3 Veneration of the Living-Dead and Zulu Anthroponymy	68
4 Names and Social Identity in the Zulu Naming System	81
5 The Articulation of Conflict in Zulu Anthroponyms	102
6 Penthonyms as Reflections of Social Behaviour Patterns	124
Conclusion	137
Appendix: Names in KwaMambulu	147
Select Bibliography	157
General Index	169
Index of Personal Names	173

Acknowledgements

I am greatly indebted to my maternal grandmother, Fikisiwe Thembeni Ngidi (MaChamane), for her support, encouragement and words of wisdom that have stuck with me to this point. Unfortunately, she was called home too soon. Continue to rest in peace Ntombi kaSibeko!

My mother, Jabulile Thembekile Ngidi, for being a good role model and my daughter, Thokola Zungu, for always being the wind beneath my wings.

Ngibonga ngokwelula mantombazane!

Introduction

When I was growing up, I was always fascinated by the stories that my grandmother used to tell about her in-laws' names, which were sometimes provocative, as in the name Bhekamafa (having your eye on everyone's inheritance) and unambiguous, as in the name Buzakunyoko (literally translated, this name means 'ask your mother'). These names have a literal translation, as well as an underlying reason, depending on the circumstances under which they were given. The analysis of these naming practices and the reasons behind the names form the major part of this book.

My late grandmother, Fikisiwe Thembeni Ngidi, was of the Chamane clan in KwaMambulu. She married Mphenyi Ngidi when she was just sixteen years old, the first of his three wives. He could not provide for his wives, except for the one he found when he arrived in Johannesburg to work in the gold mines in the late 1950s. His first two wives were struggling with children in rural KwaZulu-Natal while his new wife lived a better life in the township where Mphenyi had bought her a house and provided for her children.

My grandmother had seven children; the late Mvuseni, the late Mzikayifani Emmanuel, Jabulile Thembekile (my mother), Mzwandile Samuel, the late Dumisani Mthandeni, Sibongile Patience and Nkosinathi Dumisani. My grandmother told me a fascinating story regarding the naming of Dumisani Mthandeni. Her mother-in-law, Mandoni Ngidi (MaGumede), renamed him Dunusel'umkhumbane (showing your butt to the Mkhumbane area). This was mainly because her husband, Hloshana Ngidi, had abandoned her and lived at uMkhumbane until his death, without his family knowing where he was until years after he was buried. Hloshana had told everybody in his family that he would leave for good because his wife did not respect him and was always shouting at him or insulting him for no reason. Because Mandoni was long past childbearing age, she decided to bestow this name on her grandchild. This obviously did not sit well with my grandmother, who preferred the names that her son already had. Thereafter, there was tension between my grandmother and her mother-in-law, both women thinking that they had a right to name my uncle. My grandmother would call him Mthandeni (love him) and her mother-in-law would call him Dunusela (short for Dunusel'umkhumbane).

Many of my grandmother's peers married in the same way and most suffered the same way. When her husband died, she decided to move to a mission community in KwaMaphumulo, so that her children could have better opportunities. That decision helped to disrupt the pattern of early marriages for my mother and her siblings and they all attended school and went on to tertiary institutions.

This is the main reason why I wanted to become a voice for women in similar situations through my writing. I know women in polygynous marriages suffer because of what polygyny demands from them emotionally and psychologically. They try to keep and honour the century-old tradition in the twenty-first century, but it is demanding, with one foot in ancient times, one in the contemporary world. They find this set-up beneficial when the husband provides equally and gives each wife a lavish life. However, it becomes problematic when he has a favourite wife and becomes emotionally unavailable to other wives.

KwaMambulu is a deep rural area overlooking the uThukela River. The lifestyle is still largely traditional. I chose to do my research in this area because it is where my grandmother grew up. Although she moved away, she still has relatives and a connection to this area. Most importantly, in KwaMambulu, polygyny is still practised and the names given to children reflect social dynamics within family set-ups. These days, as more and more people move to cities and are living among people of different social and cultural backgrounds, the younger generation will soon not know these names, let alone their meanings. Most of these names will be forgotten and the naming process will lose its value, resulting in Zulu names simply becoming labels.

Culture

As a result of the complexity of culture as a concept, scholars have come up with a number of definitions. Stuart Bate defines culture 'as something shared by a group of people and learned by an individual from the society. It is made out of patterns which guide behaviour and which are transmitted in a tradition that is open and adaptive and a culture designed for living' (1995: 220). Since there is no consensus on the meaning of culture, it is difficult to see how one definition of culture could satisfy all those who speak about it from the variety of disciplines they represent. For that reason, each definition has its own limitations. According to Jane Cowan, Marie-Bénédicte Dembour and Richard Wilson:

> Culture is now understood as historically produced rather than static; unbounded rather than bounded and integrated; contested rather than consensual, incorporated within structures of power such as the construction of hegemony; rooted in practices, symbols, habits, patterns of practical mastery and practical rationality within cultural categories of meaning rather than any simple dichotomy between ideas and behaviour; and negotiated and constructed through human action rather than super-organic forces (2001: 41).

Aylward Shorter acknowledges the classic definition given by E.B. Taylor, that culture is 'that complex whole which includes knowledge, belief, art, morals, law, custom and any other capabilities and habits acquired by man as a member of society' (1988: 4). However, in this fundamentally descriptive definition, human society becomes the human criterion of culture. Shorter defines culture as that which human beings learn or acquire as members of society. He argues that culture is made up of learned aspects, as opposed to inherited aspects of human thinking and behaviour. It includes how they dress, their marriage customs and family life, their patterns of work, religious ceremonies and leisure pursuits.

Language and culture

This book recognises the Sapir-Whorf hypothesis (Whorf 1956: 57), a linguistic relativity principle, which theorises that thought and behaviour are determined and partially influenced by language. It is founded on two main ideas: the first is a theory of determinism that states that the language one speaks determines the way you will interpret the world around you. The second states that language influences your thoughts about the real world. Language and culture are interdependent entities. 'Culture' for African people is deeply embedded in the language they speak, which means that culture is part of their language.

J.F. Downs (1971: 30–1) argues that 'the ability to symbolise, to make one thing stand for something else, is what makes man unique. With the use of symbols, and especially human language, which can be seen as a systematic arrangement of sounds and meaning', culture is transmitted to future generations. Language makes it possible to teach other people the results of experiences they might never have themselves. Bartley Tengan states:

> In some respect, language and culture do exist as separate structured entities and should be identified as such, while in other respects, language becomes embedded in culture acting as the link between cultural practices and the mental creativity of human society. In theory, the descriptive meaning of language and culture and the functional relationship that is being established between them will always be different depending on which aspects of human behaviour and mental creativity are under consideration (cited in Saarelma-Maunumaa 2003: 36).

According to Ronald Langacker (1994: 26), language and culture are neither separate nor identical entities, but they overlap extensively, and both are facets of cognition. Herbert Landar (1966: 130) states that language is a set of habits concerning sign behaviour, whereas culture is the total set of human habits.

Acculturation

Acculturation is influenced by several factors, one of which is the fact that many people are moving to urban areas, where they live in multilingual and multicultural communities. When culture changes, so does the language, which then leads to changes in naming practices.

E. Adamson Hoebel argues that the 'acculturating society alters its culture in the direction of adjustment and (greater or lesser) conformity to cultural ideology and patterns of dominant society' (cited in Saarelma-Maunumaa 2003: 24). Acculturation is always a complex process and the actual evolution of the culture of particular societies is an adaptive process through which a society solves problems with respect to the natural and to the human environment. The environments are so diverse, the problems so numerous, and the solutions potentially so various that no single determinant can be equally powerful for all cases.

In Zulu culture, acculturation is evident in the embrace of Western culture and changes in the naming process. Some Zulu people are moving away from names with negative meanings, even though those names were given to them with a protective intention (see Chapter 5 for a full discussion).

Polygamy

The term 'polygamy' is used in related ways in social anthropology and sociobiology. In social anthropology, polygamy is the practice of marriage to more than one spouse simultaneously (as opposed to monogamy where each person has only one spouse at a time). In sociobiology, polygamy is used in a broad sense to mean any form of multiple mating. Mushir Hosain Kidwai notes that polygamy was never forbidden or even curtailed or regulated by Jesus Christ or his immediate apostles. Kidwai says: 'Polygamy prevailed among Christians for ages after Christ. That Christendom today claims to be monogamous is due not to Christianity but to social reformation. It had been an established institution from time immemorial. No religious or social system condemned it' (n.d.: 2).

Despite this long history, Marvin Harris (1988: 311) argues that polygamy overlooks the fact that plural marriages create domestic situations that are behaviourally and mentally very different from those created by monogamous marriages.

Polygamy exists in three specific forms: polygyny (one man having multiple wives); polyandry (one woman having multiple husbands); and group marriage (some combination of polygyny or polyandry). Polygyny is by far the most common form of polygamy.

Polyandry

In some African societies polyandry is allowed and it is normal practice for women to have more than one husband. A notable example of polyandry elsewhere in the world occurs in the Hindu culture in the Mahabharata, where the Pandavas are married to one common wife, called the Draupadi. Today, it is almost exclusively observed in the Toda tribe of India, where it is sometimes the custom for several brothers to have one wife. In this context, the practice is intended to keep land from being split up among male heirs. Polyandry was traditionally practised among nomadic Tibetans, where it meant two brothers shared a wife (Lewis 2020). It is important to note that in the research area this form of polygamy is grossly under-researched. Polygyny is more commonly known and is also more widely accepted. A woman with more than one partner is most often regarded as promiscuous.

Polygyny and gender balance

This form of polygamy is most common in African countries, although some people question whether polygyny is safe in the era of HIV and AIDS, especially on the African continent. However, Sam Mcetywa argues:

> The AmaMpondo practice polygamous marriages. It could be mistaken to conclude that polygamy promotes the spread of HIV/AIDS because of the assumption that all such marriages are untrustworthy. Like any heterosexual marriage, traditional polygamous marriage is sacred, solemn and trustworthy. Tradition has laid down principles to protect such marriages from STDs and HIV/AIDS. Such rules are known by the whole society who monitors that they are followed. It is only when the rules are broken that such diseases can come in. Therefore, it is not the practice of polygamy that brings HIV/AIDS but the misuse of tradition that needs to be dealt with (cited in Phiri and Tembo 2004: 11).

Philippe Denis asserts that polygamy may in fact be a deterrent in the spread of HIV: 'Polygamy is not dangerous from an AIDS point of view if the man limits his sexual contacts to his wives, while wives have no sexual activity outside marriage. This could account, at least partly, for the low incidence of HIV in predominantly Muslim countries such as Senegal and Mali' (cited in Oliello 2005: 82). However, this argument is based on that 'if'. There is no guarantee that the husband will be faithful to his wives, or that his wives will be faithful to their husband. Walter Trobisch (1971: 31–2) argues that those who view polygyny as an antidote against adultery see only one part of the problem. Once an inclusive sex partnership is accepted, the first step towards adultery is taken because a husband usually stays with one wife for a week at a time, or with the favourite wife for a long time. As a result, he is not able to sexually satisfy all his wives. Polygynists have a great burden in meeting the needs of plural unions. The husband has difficulty in striving to provide an equitable distribution of his love. The relationship between a husband and his wives is always tenuous, as he sometimes does not have enough time to pay attention to each of them, as should be the case.

I have reservations about believing that parties in polygynous marriages can be faithful and trustworthy, and I do not have faith in the effectiveness of traditional laws and rules surrounding fidelity in marriage. As far back as 1958, Gunnar Helander made a case for monogamy, saying: 'Today, unfortunately, in the towns and to some extent in the country, the old stability of African marriage has vanished' (1958: 21).

In most polygynous cultures, women are regarded as inferior to men and male dominance is the norm because the man is the head of the household:

> It is indeed in the rights of women, and the respect for personality, that monogamy has one of its surest justifications. Where there are several wives there is bound to creep in an idea of the inferiority of women, who tend to be regarded as property, or as lower beings (Parrinder: 1958: 35).

This view is widely held by a variety of scholars. For example, Musimbi Kanyoro argues that polygyny is an institution that is oppressive to women and it thrives in a patriarchal culture, which is based on the superiority of males. She states: 'Polygamy has tended to exploit women and child labour because polygamy is justified as a means of enhancing productivity of property for the man. Polygamy also depicts women as weak and needing constant protection' (2002: 5). Other African authors also believe that polygyny is oppressive to women: 'The promotion and encouragement of polygamy were based on grounds that favoured men by boosting their personality and reducing that of women to subservient and inferior status. The whole system supported and enhanced men's power and domination over women' (Nasimiyu-Wasike and Mugambi 1992: 107).

Polygyny as a global practice
According to the 'Ethnographic Atlas Code Book' (Gray 1998), taking on more than one wife requires considerable resources. This may put polygamy beyond the means of the vast majority of people. Such appears to be the case in many traditional Islamic societies. Within polygynous societies, multiple wives often become a status symbol, denoting wealth and power. Similarly, within societies that formally prohibit polygamy, social opinion may look favourably on people maintaining mistresses or engaging in serial monogamy. According to the 'Ethnographic Atlas Codebook' (Gray 1998), 186 cultures were monogamous in 1980; 453 had occasional polygyny; 588 had more frequent polygyny and only 4 had polyandry.

Women's rights
After the period of second-wave feminism in the 1960s to 1980s, there were changes in attitude towards sexual morality and behaviour: women were more in control of their bodies and increasingly able to experience sex with more freedom than was previously socially acceptable. This sexual revolution was seen as positive (especially by sex-positive feminists), as it enabled women and men to experience sex in a free and equal manner. However, some feminists feel that the results of the sexual revolution were only beneficial to men. Some believe that the institution of marriage is oppressive to women. Those that hold this view opt for cohabitation or, more recently, to live independently, resorting to casual sex to fulfil their sexual needs.

For the feminist, polygamy was, and still is, an exploitation of women and their rights. There is mass poverty in African societies and not every man can afford to be polygamous. It goes without saying that some men still become polygynists, knowing well that they cannot afford more wives. More people have been educated into Western standards and values, whereas traditional African society was more community-oriented and less selfish. Today, more and more people are concerned with having enough to eat and enough money to spend on themselves, which is individualistic and selfish from an African point of view.

The polygynous system is more for the benefit of male sexual needs than those of women. It disregards what is important to women. If a woman is unhappy in a relationship, some people look at her as being demanding and disrespectful of her husband. Despite the high divorce rates in monogamous marriages, it at least shows that people have a choice as to how they want to live their lives. They can marry, get divorced and remarry. They can repeat this cycle as many times as they wish.

Polygyny, according to feminists, objectifies women. The difference in status between co-wives also causes these women to fight (verbally or physically) for their ultimate prize, which, in this case, is their husband. To the feminist, the paying of *ilobolo* for the bride gives the husband power over these women. They become his property because he 'bought' them. Feminists argue that this causes women to lose their self-respect and self-esteem and devalues them. The issue of sterile and fertile wives also concerns feminists because the former end up being ostracised and called names. The same applies to the first wife who cannot have a son; all the inheritance she is entitled to goes to the next wife if she has a son. This suggests that women are always at the mercy of their husbands.

Because of the role some women play in today's economy, their holding high positions of power can cause many African male polygynists to feel inadequate. Formerly, the polygynist's strong hold on their not-so-well-educated African women stemmed from the fact that women were the only 'object' towards which the male could direct that power. The polygynist now generally feels powerless against the economic power above him – often white male economic power. Many educated people believe that having a nuclear family is appropriate because the cost of living is so high. They argue that one cannot afford to have a big family and they limit family gatherings to a minimum to try to cut costs. Nowadays, family members cannot arrive unannounced as they could in the past. The emphasis on economising and keeping the family as small as possible is evident in the names of children with educated parents, such as Kwanele (that is enough) and Aphelele (enough girls or boys).

Reasons African men give for being polygynists

Polygynists I interviewed during the course of my research argued that African men have practised polygyny in African society for centuries and it was not until the Christian missionaries came that it became taboo. A man's wealth was, and in some cases still is, measured by the number of wives and children he has. Polygyny is a form of marriage that brings the greatest number of children. Men generally prefer polygyny because it gives them sexual gratification and diversity of mates. In most African societies, it is taboo for a couple to engage in sexual intercourse during the woman's menstrual period and during pregnancy. Polygyny is seen as providing a solution for a man whose wife is either menstruating or pregnant. In agricultural societies, human labour was, and still is, essential and polygyny provided more hands to work in the fields, thus producing more food. The arguments for polygyny are that it produces wealth and stability for the entire family and women and children are safer in larger households where they are better protected from aggressors. Pride is associated with a larger family and shame and low self-esteem are associated with small families, which are often perceived as symptoms of poverty.

To the surprise of many people, polygyny provides a form of birth control, in the sense that it allows for the spacing of children by virtue of the sexual taboos attached to sex during breastfeeding. Polygyny also ensures that most marriageable girls are married. In most traditional African societies, the custom of levirate marriage and widow inheritance still exists, where a man's wife is passed on to his brother or cousin after his death. This is designed to ensure that no widows or orphans are left without provision and family. In addition, supporters of polygyny argue that it avoids the hypocritical behaviour prevalent in Western societies where many marriages fall apart because of infidelities. John Mbiti maintains:

> Polygamy helps to prevent or reduce unfaithfulness and prostitution, especially on the part of the husband. This is particularly valuable in modern times when men generally go to live and work in the cities and towns, leaving their children in the rural area. If the husband has several wives, he can afford to take one at a time to live with him in the town while the other wife remains behind to take care of the children and family property in the countryside (1969: 139).

This statement corresponds with life in most traditional African societies where men are given more sexual rights than women. According to Anne Nasimiyu-Wasike, nothing in a polygamous marriage is intended to benefit women: 'The reasons that are used to justify polygamy in traditional Africa reveal a distorted relationship that has crippled both women and men in different ways' (cited in Oliello 2005: 79). Mbiti further points out: 'Polygamy also raises the social status of the family concerned. It is instilled in the minds of the African people that a big family earns its head great respect in the eyes of the community' (1969: 139). Often it is the rich families that are made up of polygamous marriages. If the first wife has no children, or if she has only daughters, it follows almost without exception that her husband will add another wife, partly to remedy the immediate concern of being without a male child, and partly to remove the shame and anxiety of apparent unproductivity. Each marriage is expected to ensure the continuation of the extended family and clan. There is a belief in some African societies that those who die are reborn in their children. Therefore, it is important to have children to perpetuate the family line.

Mbiti also argues: 'Marriage and procreation in African communities are a unit. Without procreation, marriage is incomplete' (1969: 133). This was confirmed during my research: having children is vitally important; a woman who cannot conceive is shunned and called names, like *inyumba* or *ubhonya* (the barren one).

Benezeri Kisembo, Laurenti Magesa and Aylward Shorter, explaining the view of the people of East Africa regarding children, explain:

> Very common in East Africa was the concept of nominal reincarnation, the custom of naming children after grandparents

and even referring to them by regularly alternating kinship terms. The verbal practice was backed by the belief that a special relationship existed between grandparents and the grandchild and that grandparents acted as guardian spirit or protector of the child . . . It can be readily understood that childlessness placed a very heavy if not intolerable strain upon a marriage. Without the alternative of polygamy, divorce would be practically inevitable (1977: 73).

They also argue that polygyny is seen to increase the labour force and assists in food production (Kisembo, Magesa and Shorter 1977: 68). Seen in this light, a large family community renders all the operations of rural life more efficiently. It also makes co-operation in communal work less demanding, since there are more representatives of the family available to participate.

In African traditional society, polygyny is seen to provide for unbroken continuation of the family, for both the husband and the children in the event of the death of one wife. The husband would not experience loneliness and other difficulties because the other wife would be there for him, and the children would not struggle as much because another mother would be there. Mbiti explains this view when he notes:

> When a family is made up of several wives with their households, it means that in time of need, there will always be someone around to help. This is a corporate existence, for example, when one wife dies, there are others to take care of her children. In case of sickness, other wives will fetch water from the river, cut firewood and cook (1969: 143).

Polygyny caters for the desire of having a larger family, and in most traditional African societies parents have as many children as is physically possible. Children belong not only to the nuclear household, but also to the extended family and the community. Another important issue is having male children. A man desires that his name and family line will be continued, hence he feels it essential to have a male child. If he has no male child by his first wife, he then takes a second wife, thinking that she will produce a male child. Polygyny is also seen to provide for the loss of children through sickness and death. In addition, polygyny can act as a deterrent against divorce. For example, Babs Fafunwa asserts:

> An African finds that there are more divorce cases in America, where people marry but one. In Africa, men have the privilege of marrying two or more wives, all depending on the husband's economic backstay. He also finds that American women are more jealous than their African counterparts when it comes to love affairs (cited in Bhengu 1975: 77).

African traditionalists argue that people cannot accept the institution of marriage without at least recognising the existence of polygyny. The fundamental character of polygamy in African society is borne out by the fact that this form of African marriage is the base of the extended family, which is the backbone of African communal relations and living.

Polygyny in South Africa

Polygyny is prevalent in rural communities in South Africa and is encouraged by the fact that in patriarchal cultures women of marriageable age must get married. This puts unnecessary pressure on women to find marriage partners, even if it is to men who are already married. For older wives who have lost their desire for sex, their husband taking on more and younger wives may seem to be a solution. Co-wives live in constant fear of contracting HIV as no protection is used during intercourse. There are no negotiations about sexual practices between husbands and wives in traditional societies. Sexual intercourse is for the gratification of the men and not the women. Infidelity – for men – is condoned and accepted under the banner of polygyny and culture. These types of marriages highlight gender inequality in traditional societies, in which men dominate women and the society favours male supremacy. This enforces unequal power relations already prevalent in polygynous families. With marriage considered an important milestone in women's lives, polygyny is often unavoidable for the women in these societies. It must be noted that polygyny can be sororal (where wives are related) and non-sororal (where wives are not related).

Names and language

There is a close relationship between a language and a society in which names are found. Peter Raper says: 'Language may be described as a social instrument used by members of society to communicate with one another' (1986: 1). Naming has a particular place in language systems, but it also forms part of the larger social and cultural context in which a particular language is found, as Mbali Machaba points out: 'Although names are found in a language, they do not only function as linguistic items. The fact that naming is not simply a linguistic matter, but a social and psychological matter, is demonstrated by various naming practices adopted by people from different cultural and religious backgrounds' (2005: 29). According to Ihechukwu Madubuike: 'Names are used to identify people. Onomatologists have discovered that the study of names of a given people will reveal a body of knowledge about them that other sciences may not reveal . . . Anthropologists have derived useful cultural information about people whose names they have studied' (1976: 8).

Proper names versus common nouns

Names form an important part of a language. M.T. Chauke says that 'names are historical witnesses, like very old buildings or old trees. Together with other historical data they may help to uncover a country's history' (cited in Machaba 2005: 26). Alan Gardiner makes a clear distinction between words and names: 'When we speak of a "word" our minds travel from the sound-sign to whatever it may mean; when we speak of a "name" we imply that there exists something to which a certain sound-sign corresponds' (1957: 7). Names are sometimes used without prior knowledge of their meaning, whereas words are usually used with a clear understanding of what they mean. This is particularly true with proverbial names. People use personal names all the time, but only a few are concerned with the meaning of the name.

W.F.H. Nicolaisen (1976: 144) says that the distinction between words and names lies in the difference between meaning and function: words mean and names function. The function of a name is to uniquely identify an entity. He also points out that words clearly have a much lower survival rate than names, a fact that increases the value of toponymic raw material to the scholar, the further back we go in history and prehistory.

Naming practices

Throughout the world, the naming of people varies and carries meaning, revealing much about a society. Richard Alford writes that 'ethnographic research has failed to reveal a single society which does not bestow personal names on its members' (1988: 1). Nobody is without a name. Naming is as old as time and is intimately linked to the people, their culture and religion. Nicolaisen also observes this and says further:

> In fact, naming is so intimately linked with the history of the human race and its mastery over the world by which it is surrounded, that ultimately the history of naming may be said to be the same as the history of the human spirit or, putting it in a proverbial nutshell, man always has been, and still is, a naming animal (1976: 143).

Behind the concept of onomastics (the study of the history and origin of proper names, especially personal names) lies an utterly absorbing subject that tells us about the history, geography, traditions and culture of different societies. It is therefore important to understand the context within which names are found. Sihawukele Emmanuel Ngubane defines onomastics as: 'The study of names involving a variety of complex naming techniques. Onomastics as a science has no ending but is open-ended, accommodating new thoughts and innovations through naming in any of the languages of the people of the earth' (2000: 17). Through onomastics one looks at a name, sees the literal meaning and then goes further and examines the story behind that name to find out more about the name-bearer, their immediate and extended family, and the community at large.

The work on personal names by Willy van Langendonck (1983, 1987) sheds valuable light on the use of semantic-pragmatic theory in the characterisation of personal names. Van Langendonck observes: 'Personal names constitute the most diversified category of proper names. Proper nouns and pronouns are referential means par excellence, more than common nouns' (1990: 1). He maintains that primary names are those that fulfil the three functions of personal names: 'Address (talk to), identification (talk about) and a wide possibility of subcategorisation as to gender and expressivity (especially combinability with diminutive and augmentative morphemes)' (Van Langendonck 2001: 204).

In his comparative analysis, Adrian Koopman (1986) compares the concept and the use of Zulu names to those of other societies, particularly other black societies in Africa. This is one of the earliest studies to investigate why parents name their children as they do and their reasons clearly show links between naming and social dynamics. His category of 'friction names' is similar to the discussion of names in Chapter 4 of this book. In Zulu societies there are different types of names: anthroponymy is the study of anthroponyms, the proper names of human beings, personal names, nicknames and personal praises. Secondly, Koopman discusses surnames, clan names and clan praises. Thirdly, he discusses the standardisation of spelling, semantics and the historico-cultural background of Zulu place names. Elsewhere, he also examines school names, names of homesteads and shop names (Koopman 2002). He later highlights the uniqueness of the Zulu anthroponymic system. He speaks of the fact that some names are not chosen from the existing Zulu anthroponymicon (vocabularly for naming) – for example, a name like Sipho, which is found in almost every village, whereas names like Qinisela (persevere) are unique and rare (Koopman 1989).

A study conducted by Carol Lombard (2008) indicates that in the Canadian Niitsitapi (Blackfoot Indians), personal names play a major role in capturing and conveying various aspects of traditional Niitsitapi sociocultural knowledge. Niitsitapi personal names thus appear to form an integral part of the Niitsitapi oral tradition and play a powerful role in establishing and maintaining Niitsitapi conceptualisations of individuals, as well as their social and cultural identity. Lombard is of the opinion that, in addition to their nominative function, names contain and communicate sociocultural meaning based on their associations with a wide range of non-linguistic factors, which form part of the sociocultural environment within which they are used.

Shona anthroponyms are an example of language use for specific purposes. Livingstone Makondo (2009) examines the period of 1890 to 2006 and explores how linguistics can be used to glean the intended and implied meaning(s) of various first names. He recognises current dominant given name categories and establishes eleven broad factors behind the use of given names. He goes on to identify 24 broad-based, theme-oriented categories, envisaged naming trends and name categories. His study indicates the nature of names Shona people prefer, as well as their preferred address forms. Makondo posits that Shona first names resulted from the unparalleled anthroponomastic and linguistic innovation displayed by the Shona people. War names play a vital role not only in concealing the old identity of the guerrillas in Zimbabwe, but also in creating new identities, which were used as weapons for challenging the enemy and contesting space (Pfukwa 2007).

Names are sometimes used as guidelines and describe some of the words and symbols used that are essential in typical naming ceremonies. For example, Kokunre Agbontaen-Eghafona (2007) discusses the importance of indigenous names in southern Nigerian society in understanding the values of the people.

R. Gamble (1996) discusses two studies that were conducted on the academic records of 4 497 black South African schoolchildren in first and second grade from 1989 to 1994. The first study was a hierarchical, multiple-regression analysis, which found no significant relationship between the popularity of a given name and the academic achievement of first grade black South African schoolchildren. The second study Gamble conducted was an analysis of variance between the discrepancy means of random pairs of pupils in any classroom and the discrepancy means of pairs of pupils with the same name in the same classroom. His main finding was that individual teachers in some classrooms positively stereotype pupils with the same name.

Naming practices in Zulu culture

Culture includes knowledge, beliefs, morals and any other capabilities and habits acquired by a person as a member of society. Culture is linked to the language people speak because culture and beliefs are communicated through language. The language used in name-giving is reflective of the cultural and religious beliefs of the parents who gave the names. Cultural changes have brought about shifts in society's thinking and have affected naming processes.

Co-wives often express their unhappiness and frustration through names. The articulation of discontent through the use of language and the choice of personal names that reflect the translation of ideas and feelings of the name-giver are evident in the Zulu naming process. These chosen names accommodate events prescribed by the society and are culturally permissible. These articulations are commonly used in rural communities, but also echo in urban social settings. Hostility and ill-feelings are thus channelled through the sanctioned form of these various oral expressions, either as a means of merely airing one's dissatisfaction or as a means of seeking personal redress (Turner 2003). Zulu people consider the state of their affairs and their well-being before naming their children. Through names, language meets culture (daily living routines) and religion (beliefs regulating people's lives). Names reflect how people relate to one another and also detail the grievances and issues they have against one another.

Simon A. Roberts (1979) mentions research that shows that people in African communal societies are extremely sensitive, not only to ridicule, but even to the mildest criticism. This influences people to adhere to approved patterns of behaviour. Roberts maintains:

> In any small closely knit community where people find themselves in continuing face-to-face relations, the threat of exposure to ridicule and disgust, provoking feelings of shame and remorse must represent an important mechanism of control . . . Almost all these means of maintaining order, particularly those which derive their force from the actor's perception of how other people may react, operate through human communication in the course of everyday life. Through talk, values and norms may be expressly stated, and consequences of departure from them spelled out (1979: 42).

When giving names, parents look at their relationships with the immediate or extended family and the community at large. They consider their status in the community and their relationship with God or the Creator. Through names, an outsider can easily detect the kind of relationships that family members have. If there is constant bickering and arguing within the family, this is reflected in the names given to children born around or during the time of the event that is the source of argument. This becomes more pronounced in traditional polygynous families because women 'officially' share their husband and squabbles are frequent in such settings.

This book examines the names of children within polygynous families not only because the stories behind them are usually intriguing but also, and more importantly, because they clearly reflect the relationship between the living and the living-dead. The living-dead are (to a Zulu person) intermediaries between the living and the dead and they command great respect. The term 'living-dead' was originally used by Mbiti (1970: 10) to describe ancestors in Africa. It has since been generally adopted by scholars and representatives of traditional African religions. James Amanze provides the background to the term: 'To many African people the dead people are not dead at all. Death is only a transitional state to a spiritual life free from material hindrances. The deceased are at once dead and alive, and because of their paradoxical nature they are known as the living-dead' (2003: 44). Johannes Triebel (2002: 188) mentions that in Africa the living-dead are part of the reality of life. Their existence and reality are unquestioned and they are still seen to influence those on earth, both in good and bad ways. The ancestors therefore remain still part of the community of the living and, as such, 'the living-dead' is an apt term.

The respect people have for their living-dead forces them to always be on their best behaviour. The living-dead are watchdogs of peace within the family, which means people cannot voice their anger by shouting at each other because this might anger the living-dead. Angering the living-dead may cause them to stop watching over the family, which may then lead to calamities, such as unexplained illnesses. If a family member falls ill, they may go to a conventional Western medical doctor, who may say that there is nothing wrong with them. The person may continue to feel ill until they decide to consult a diviner (*isangoma*) who will communicate with the living-dead on their behalf. The living-dead will then shed light on the problem and advise the *isangoma* on the kind of herbs to use to cure the person. Sometimes people consult an *inyanga* (herbalist) who, after throwing bones, will be able to discern what is wrong with the person.

Relationships with the living-dead must thus be maintained at all costs in order to have peace within a homestead. According to

H.M. Thipa (1983) a name may show that nature has a way of compensating the parents who have lost a child – seen, for example, in the names Sibuyiselwe (we have been given back what was taken from us), Nkosiyangithanda (the Lord loves me) and Philangomusa (we are alive because of his mercy). Survival names belong mainly to men and young men. This might be because men are believed to keep homes running and protected and to carry on the family name. These names are M-commencing commands that end with *-ni* (plural suffix). They are directed to a group of people, evil spirits and the ancestors, and they contain clear instruction of what needs to be done.

How African people view death, and what happens thereafter, is crucial to the way they behave in and around the homestead, and in the manner in which they conduct themselves when they have disagreements. The fact that African people perceive their deceased relatives as playing a big role in their own lives keeps the living family members in line. Mbiti (1969: 153) claims:

> There is the real cessation of part of the person at death, so that he 'sleeps' but never to wake up again. Death is cruel, it 'stiffens', 'cuts down' or 'evaporates' a person, even if he continues to exist in the hereafter. This cruelty of death comes out in funeral dirges. African people feel privileged that they have people they know who can channel their grievances to the Almighty, however, they do not perceive the process of passing away as an achievement in itself. At the time it happens they see it as a loss, but later see it as an advantage.

It should be noted that though some Zulu societies still bury their dead in and around the homesteads, people have a choice of using graveyards for burial and also have a choice to cremate them. Death is something that disturbs harmonious living in traditional communities. It also commands a longer mourning period, where people cannot do as they please because death is a highly respected event in the community.

Names are used to avoid confrontation between family members who have disagreements. For example, the name Yekezakhe (not worried about her own affairs) was given to a boy whose mother felt that her co-wife was too concerned about what was happening in her (the mother's) household. Names within polygynous families are an indirect commentary or reaction about sociocultural deeds in a society at the time of the birth of the name-bearer. For example, the name Fikelephi (what kind of a place did she arrive at?) was given to a girl whose mother was worried about the unhealthy environment her little girl had been born into. The names criticise, admonish, praise or explain a course of action by family members and are used as strategic alternatives to confrontational discourse. Another example is in the name Hlushwayini (why have you made this your business?), given to a girl whose mother was tired of her in-laws giving her advice on how to do things, so she was sarcastically asking them why her decisions bother them since she was the one who was going to have to live with the consequences.

Samuel Gyasi Obeng comments on names within polygynous families:

> African names are reactions to potentially difficult communicative situations and therefore involve indirectness . . . names within polygynous families have the capacity to express the thoughts of the members of society, especially the thoughts of the parents of the child, more forcefully and louder than plain or direct speech because they 'respond' to specific, potentially difficult, social or political issues common in the society and the response is 'permanent' for as long as the individual lives (2001: 49).

Women in polygynous marriages often feel trapped and voiceless; they accept polygyny even though they find it oppressive. These women feel that getting married changes them into objects of procreation. When a woman cannot bear a son, she becomes an object of ridicule within the clan. These women use names to voice their feelings and to share their experiences with the society (Zondi 2012).

Names form an integral part of Zulu culture in that each person has a name and that name becomes that person. It is believed the sorcerers use people's names to bewitch them. The sorcerers may use people's names at night while using *umuthi* (traditional medicine) that will cause them to become ill. Consequently, it is believed that there are many illnesses that are the result of sorcerers using people's names to bewitch them.

Names are used to express anger and frustration and to let people know if they have done something wrong. Names sometimes refer to the 'state of mind' of the parents. Koopman notes:

> Names referring to the 'state of mind' of the parents in the central reaches of Africa are frequently negative. Such names refer to the constant imminence of sorrow, death, poverty or misfortune. In societies which see frequent stillbirth, or loss of a child in its early years, as well as the jealousy of neighbours, co-wives, or ancestral spirits, it is not uncommon for the child to be given a name which means 'who wants him?', 'turn your back on him' or 'cast him out'. Such names are meant to mislead the 'jealous powers' into thinking that it will be no harm to the parents to take the child away, as it is unwanted anyway. A variation of this thinking is seen when a far greater proportion of boy children are lost in birth or in their early days (2002: 39).

Zulu people sometimes use family genealogies in bestowing names on their children, as discussed by Susan M. Suzman (2002). People give names according to their social status – for example, names given by the family of a nurse married to a teacher, as in the name Nomfundo (mother of education), or names given by the family of a poor woman with no husband. According to Mbali Shabalala (1999), homestead names reflect social dynamics in the Mabengela community near Nkandla in KwaZulu-Natal. Shabalala pays particular attention to the reasons for name-giving and examines the unique way in which these names reflect social behaviour patterns within the society in which they are found.

There has been a change in the Zulu anthroponymic systems. As Ellie Khumalo (2007) argues, names with enclitics like *-phi?* (where), as in the name Sholiphi (which one are you talking about?) and *-ni?* (what), as in the name Bathini (what are they saying?) are no longer favoured by Zulu people.

African religion and the philosophy behind it

The naming of a person in Africa is a spiritual event. Most African societies have a naming ceremony, which they perceive as sacred and religious. Naming is, therefore, part of their religion. They believe that the living-dead have everything to do with what occurs in their lives; the good (as a reward for good behaviour) and the bad (as a punishment for misbehaviour). Mbiti (1969: 1) claims:

> Africans are notoriously religious, and each people has its own religious system with a set of beliefs and practices. Religion permeates into all the departments of life so fully that it is not easy or possible always to isolate it... To ignore these traditional beliefs, attitudes and practices, can only lead to a lack of understanding of African behaviour and problems. Religion is the strongest element in traditional background and exerts probably the greatest influence upon the thinking and living of the people concerned.

Witchcraft

Geoffrey Parrinder (1954: 125) writes that witchcraft is nocturnal; the witch is supposed to go out only at night when her body is asleep and she preys on other souls that are wandering while their bodies are asleep. Since people believe that dreams are activities of the soul, which travels to the places the dreamer thinks about and meets the people they see in the dream, it is evident that a great deal of witchcraft belief depends on dreams.

In the data that was collected, there were a number of names suggesting that the belief in witchcraft is still rife in the KwaMambulu area, as can be seen in the names Felamandla (he is bewitched because he is strong), Bhekumuthi (watching the use of *umuthi*), Nyathelephi (where did you put your foot?) and Fumbetheni (what do you have in your closed hand?). It is also clear that people use personal names to perform evil deeds.

Edward Evans-Pitchard differentiates between witchcraft and sorcery: 'A witch performs no rite, utters no spell, and possesses no medicines. An act of witchcraft is a psychic act. They [the Azande] believe also that sorcerers may do them ill by performing magic rites with bad medicines' (cited in Bockie 1993: 41). Michael Bourdillon concurs and notes:

> Generally, witchcraft involves the reverse of normal values and behaviour. Witches are typically believed to act at night, instead of openly by the day as honest people do, and to operate with familiar animals of the night, such as hyenas and owls. The special powers of the witches are often assumed to come from evil spirits that encourage the witches in their evil practices . . . Witches are assumed to be able to protect themselves from revenge (cited in Olupona 2000: 176).

Witchcraft divides a society and destroys families, so people who are suspected of practising witchcraft are ostracised and treated as outlaws. It is important to try to find out why some are suspects and others not. Women are the most prone to suspicion of witchcraft. Parrinder (1954: 131) points out that conflict between wives and their mothers-in-law is prominent in accusations of witchcraft. In a polygynous household, young wives denounce their husband's mother or another wife. The wife is often a stranger in the family, having been married from another village. If she has no children, she may be suspected of jealousy. Moreover, if her own children die, she may be accused of having killed them. Or she will accuse a barren woman, a co-wife, or a mother-in-law past childbearing age of jealousy and child murder by witchcraft.

* * *

This book foregrounds matters pertaining to how names are given in Zulu society; how names are used by women as channels of communication; how culture and religion are used to subjugate women and force them to conform in polygynous families. The relationship between polygyny, religion, culture and names creates a gender dichotomy that becomes difficult for women to navigate. These patriarchal patterns subordinate women to men, as established in sociological research on different families as well as the ideologies of masculine authority that support it (Connell 1987: 122–3).

The study aims to highlight the relevance of the veneration of the living-dead in Zulu culture by dismissing assumptions that people usually make concerning Zulu personal names. People tend to pay more attention to the literal meaning of given names, which may be deceiving as it says nothing about the name-giver and the reason they might have had for bestowing that name. This book also provides insight into Zulu 'traditional' polygynous families and exposes the myths concerning polygynous families. It examines how names bestowed on children within polygynous families reflect the living conditions within such contexts. In these communities, people use names to air their concerns, as in the name Zibeleni (why are you ignoring me or the situation?).

Chapter outline

Chapter 1 discusses the integral part played by *ilobolo* and marriage in Zulu traditional societies. It gives a comprehensive meaning of *ilobolo* within the context of communities within which they are found.

The second chapter speaks to the 'culture' often used to justify polygyny, even by men who cannot afford it. It examines how polygyny is associated with gender inequalities, the subjugation of women and toxic masculinities, as it creates inequalities between co-wives. The data collected demonstrates that polygyny negates women's empowerment as it enforces women's subjugation and male dominance.

Amadlozi (ancestors) are at the core of the lives of traditional Zulu societies and are regarded as 'dead but alive' spiritual beings. Chapter 3 describes their role in the family and how this relates to the anthroponyms given to children in traditional polygynous families. It also examines the power the living-dead have on the misbehaving family members in the homestead.

Names are used to project individual identity and locate the name-bearers within the family and society. Chapter 4 focuses on the primary function of names, which is to refer to, denote and identify the name-bearers. This chapter highlights the communicative function of names, which is about the externalisation of conflict. Most importantly, it also explores how name choices act as links to polygyny, family structure and the state of mind of the parents at the time of birth.

Names are often used as a processual paradigm to maintain order in traditional societies. Chapter 5 focuses on the aetiology of Zulu anthroponyms and how they are used to air discontent, anger and disappointment. The examples from the data collected indicate how names are effective channels of communication to avoid confrontation within polygynous families.

Allegations of the practice of witchcraft and sorcery are always alluded to in traditional societies when death strikes. Parents whose children die bestow names directed to death, sorcerers and the evil spirits. Chapter 6 discusses penthonyms/death-prevention names, which are given to children to mislead the evil powers into thinking the child is not wanted. It brings to the fore the social significance of witchcraft.

Finally, the appendix provides a unique list of Zulu anthroponyms collected in KwaMambulu.

1

The Way of Life in KwaMambulu

This chapter presents background information on the research site, KwaMambulu, Kranskop, in KwaZulu-Natal. Kranskop is a small town situated on the edge of the uThukela River valley, 100 kilometres from Durban. It was founded in 1894 as Hopetown, but following confusion with another town of the same name in the Northern Cape, the name was changed. Kranskop (Afrikaans, meaning 'cliff head') was named after two cliff faces that rise 1 175 metres above the uThukela valley. The Kranskop rock formation is called Ntunjambili in isiZulu and is significant in local legend and folklore.

    The KwaMambulu area is predominantly rural and overlooks the uThukela River. Only in recent years have tarred roads and electricity reached certain areas where there is road access. Some areas are not accessible by car. About 3 000 people reside in this area, 65 per cent of whom are middle-aged and women. The youth usually move away to get an education and men leave to look for jobs. The area is ruled by a chief and about a dozen headmen. Any grievances that the inhabitants have with each other are presided over by the tribal council.

    In KwaMambulu things are done in a specific way in keeping with the rural community and their expectations. Each person knows their role in and contribution to the community. They are a traditional society and live their lives as such. They are a monolingual society, speaking isiZulu, with some members of the community understanding English. Approximately half the members of this community are Christian and half Nazareth Baptist (Shembe). The people of KwaMambulu live in autonomous homesteads (*imizi*) surrounded by fields and grazing land. Each homestead consists of several houses (usually rondavels), belonging to the co-wives and their children. The main hut at the top of the homestead belongs to the grandmother and is perceived as the sanctuary for the living-dead. Subsistence farming is done by the women, who plough the fields.

Dress code

The women in this community wear what is seen as appropriate clothing whether they are married or not. Unmarried women wear clothes that show off their breasts – breasts are not, in traditional African culture, viewed as an erogenous zone. They can also wear short traditional skirts – *izigege* (a bead belt that covers only the vulva), *onomndindi* (a very short pleated skirt made out colourful cloth) and *omabubane* (a wrap-around beaded belt) – that show off half of their thighs. This is to convey to possible future husbands that they are still virgins eligible for marriage.

In a rural community such as KwaMambulu, women still 'know their place'. There are women who are well educated and can provide for themselves, but even they still believe in respecting their husbands and taking orders from them, unlike their urban counterparts. There are many chores strictly allocated to women, such as fetching water and wood, and cooking for the household. The women kneel when giving things to their husbands, be it food, water or traditional beer.

There are two groups of women: the first are those who belong to the indigenous religious group of the Nazareth Baptist Church, or *abakwaShembe* (the followers of Isaiah Shembe). This group is very traditional and most of them are in polygynous marriages. They wear traditional attire at all times and seem to always be obedient to their husbands. These women appreciate their husbands even though they keep on taking more wives. To them, the words 'cheating' and 'divorce' do not exist because polygyny has been a way of life for them from time immemorial; they know no other life. 'A man is a man' is what one of the young wives told me. She argued that with polygyny at least you know who your rivals are and you know where your husband is when he is not with you. In her view, in monogamous marriages, a man might stray without the knowledge of his wife – he could sleep with another woman and come back pretending nothing has happened. Women in those kinds of marriages, she insisted, brag about being the only women in their husbands' lives, not knowing that their husbands are having affairs behind their backs. The most embarrassing thing about this is that the wife is often the last one to know. These traditional women prefer everything to be done with their knowledge. They might not have a say in whether their husband takes another wife, or who will be their husband's choice of a co-wife, but at least they are consulted before it happens. It is not important to them that their opinions do not matter when it comes to giving their men advice against a woman who comes from a rival family, for example, the daughter of a sorcerer. It seemed to me, as the researcher, that they felt empowered that they have control over the situation, no matter how small that control was.

The second group is made up of educated women who choose not to follow tradition; here we are talking of teachers, nurses and the like. All of them dress appropriately, with dresses or skirts below their knees. The length of the skirt says a great deal about the character of the person wearing it. The back of a woman's leg is considered to be sacred; she cannot show that off to the world. She must honour her husband and preserve his dignity in the society. No man wants his wife to be known as a loose person who has no shame. Women are not allowed to wear vests or sleeveless tops; their attire cannot be revealing or figure-hugging; and they must cover their heads with scarves or berets. This is also because these women live in big communities with their in-laws and it is inappropriate for them to show their bodies to their in-laws – it is believed that might anger the living-dead, with serious repercussions.

Food

In KwaMambulu, people prefer traditional food such as samp (*isitambu nobhontshisi*), stiff maize porridge (*phuthu*), spinach (*uphuthu nemifino*) and ground cooked dry maize (*umcaba*). Most of the food is boiled and only seasoned with salt. They seldom use cooking oil. This is not because of the fact that cooking oil causes heart disease, as I had initially thought, but because most of their staple food does not really need cooking oil and is just as good without it. Also forming part of their staple diet is sour milk or *maas* (*amasi enkomo*). There are taboos associated with certain kinds of foods. For instance, women are not allowed to eat eggs, chicken and fish because it is believed that if they do, they would be promiscuous, just like chickens and fish, because these animals are believed to be weak sexually, especially the chicken. *Omakoti* (newly married women) are not allowed to eat *maas* when they are menstruating. During this time of the month, women are avoided. They cannot have sex and they cannot go into the cattle kraal and, as a result, cannot touch anything that comes from the kraal, including milk and *maas*. This is because the cattle kraal is closely linked to the living-dead; women avoid it out of respect for the living-dead.

Umemulo *or coming of age ceremony*

Umemulo is always observed when a girl is ready to get married. Girls are told to remain virgins and abstain from sex until they are married. Girls who have reached courtship or *ukweshela* age are courted by young men. This takes place at the rivers while women are collecting water, or when they are fetching wood, or at any traditional ceremonies taking place in the community. Once the woman accepts the young man's proposal, she gives him a bead necklace (*ucu*) to symbolise her love for him. The young man is then allowed to visit the girl at her house. They can spend the night together, kiss, cuddle and caress. They can do anything to relieve themselves of sexual tension, but penetration is totally forbidden until they get married. If a woman is a virgin at the time she gets married, the young man must pay with eleven cows, but only ten cows if she is no longer a virgin (see 'The importance of paying *ilobolo*' later in this chapter).

Death

Death is a highly respected event in the community. The mourning family must use *umuthi* (traditional medicine) to cleanse themselves of bad luck after the funeral. Three months after the person has died, a cleansing ceremony is performed – *ukuxokozela* if a woman has died or *ukujikijela* if a man has died – during which men of the community go hunting before eating a slaughtered goat. A couple of months later, another ritual is performed in which a cow is slaughtered: *isihlangu* for a man or *isidwaba* for a woman. *Isihlangu* (a fighting shield) is to make sure that the man has some form of protection on his way to his living-dead. *Isidwaba* (pleated skirt made from cow hide) is to dress the woman appropriately when she goes over to the living-dead, some of whom are her in-laws. After a year, a ritual of *ukubuyisa* (bringing back the spirit of the dead) is performed to bring the spirit of the dead person home to his family.

Respect for people in positions of authority

The chief is highly respected in this community; he is the leader and everyone looks up to him. He makes the rules and he is the person to contact if negotiations with an *induna* (headman) fail. The *induna* is there to be the eyes and ears of the chief, and he attends all the occasions the chief cannot. He can decide on minor issues concerning the entire community. People report their disputes to the *induna* and if people are not satisfied with the decision, they can go to the chief for appeal, as he can overrule the *induna*'s decision.

Iphoyisa lenkosi (the chief's police officer) acts as a chief and the *induna*'s watchdog. He is the first person an outsider encounters when they visit the community. He asks them questions about their place of origin and about the business they intend conducting in the area. When there is a traditional wedding, *iphoyisa lenkosi* is the one who officiates at the ceremony on behalf of the chief. He asks the bride if she loves her husband: '*Uyabuza umthetho, uthi uyamthanda na?*' (The law is asking you: do you love him?). When a person dies, *iphoyisa lenkosi* is the one who announces the death to the community (*ukuhlaba umkhosi*). Very early on the day of the funeral, *iphoyisa lenkosi* will stand on the hill and shout at the top of his voice, saying, for instance, '*kwaNgidi eMbitane, yelekelelani, konakele*' (At the Ngidis in Mbitane, there is a crisis. Come and help out). Then people know that they need to go and help to dig the grave because somebody has passed away.

Respect in general is very important in African culture, as can be seen, for example, in the practice of *ukukhuleka* (the shouting of praise names when entering a homestead). This shows that you recognise the importance of the man of the homestead. When people come to visit, they are offered something to eat and drink. When a person offers you something to eat or drink, you take it with both hands, which is a sign of full appreciation. The person offering you food will eat with you or take a first sip from your drink to show you that it is not poisoned. It is also very common to find people drinking from one beerpot.

Linguistic features of Zulu culture and religion

African religion provides regulations for daily life through language. There is also much advice about getting on with fellow humans and the community at large in the form of sayings and proverbs – for example, *kuhlonishwana kabili* (respect is a two-way thing); *izandla ziyagezana* (hands wash each other – help those who help you); and *umuzi ngumuzi ngokuphanjukelwa* (you must treat strangers well).

Marriage is an integral part of the culture

In present-day KwaMambulu most men are still traditionalists and practise polygyny, with full knowledge (and, in rare cases, with the full support) of their first wives. Most women know that getting involved in a polygynous relationship is a challenge, as sometimes the relationship with the co-wives sours because of jealousy and the love they each have for their husband. However, many women still prefer it to monogamous marriage. They argue that a monogamous marriage does not mean that a man's sexual appetite is tamed within the marriage and they view it as better they know the women with whom they share their husband, rather than their husband having outside sexual partners who are unknown to them.

The importance of paying ilobolo

Marriage is a sacred rite of passage that involves the whole community. The paying of *ilobolo* is the most important part of the marriage negotiating process, as it involves two families and the living-dead. *Ilobolo* used to be a sign of appreciation on the husband's part. He was thanking his parents-in-law for raising and looking after his new bride-to-be. However, nowadays things have changed; people have become greedy and seek material (usually financial) benefits from this age-old tradition. The groom's family expects the bride to bring gifts for the whole family for *umabo* (distribution of gifts) during the traditional wedding ceremony, without considering the value of the money the husband's family has paid and the unnecessary financial burden they put on the bride and her family.

Consider, for example, this imagined scenario: the groom pays R15 000 to the family of the woman to be married, thinking that she is worth every penny. Her family gives her some of the money to buy things for the husband's family: she buys a kist for R5 000, caters for her husband-to-be's family when they come to her house to bring the gifts (*izibizo/amatshali*) and gives them gifts to take home (food, blankets and beverages). For the actual wedding day, she must buy *izingubo zokulala* (blankets), *amaphinifa* (aprons), *izambulela* (umbrellas), *izinkamba* (clay pots), *imicamelo* (pillows) and *amacansi* (grass mats) for the whole family, which is usually between 50 and 100 people. Additionally, she must bring dinner sets, new cooking utensils and furniture (a bedroom suite). She must stay at her mother-in-law's house for the duration of the honeymoon period and when it is time for her to move to her new house, she has to leave everything behind, except for the kist. So, all the money the husband paid as *ilobolo* goes back to his family in the end.

Most of the misconceptions about *ilobolo* come from Western people who translate it as 'bride price'. This leads to many thinking that African women have a price tag attached to them. Paying *ilobolo* has nothing to do with buying a wife. Donna M. Gelfand notes: 'The payment is a token that the husband acknowledges the benefits he is receiving. It is also a compensation for her father for the loss of his daughter, who has gone with her husband, leaving her own kin to join his' (1968: 41). The reason that many men are questioning *ilobolo* is because people have been exposed to other cultures and have adopted them. Choosing a Western tradition is an easy way out of African traditions.

Responsibilities that come with marriage
Marriage is a 'business deal'; it is an emotional and physical communication, the 'training ground' for children, and the 'survival unit' for the population at large and for humankind in general. Marriage is not just a wedding ceremony; it is a multifaceted relationship of people with common goals, but often with very different personal needs. According to John Mbiti: 'Marriage then, is a religious responsibility for everyone. It forms the focal point where departed, present and coming members of society meet. It is the point of hope and expectation for the unmarried and their relatives, once it has been reached and procreation takes place' (1969: 144). I concur with Mbiti's reasoning here because in most African societies people who fail to secure a partner are given

nicknames, as in the name Zendazamshiya (everybody is getting married and you are left behind), Mjendevu (an old maid) or Mpohlo (an unmarried man). The husband and his family transfer goods or money to the wife's family, but the words used are quite distinct from buying and selling. The transaction does not give the husband unlimited rights over his wife, as she may claim divorce for ill-treatment. And in many African communities, women are very independent.

When a woman gets married, she marries the entire clan. From *ukukhonga* (*ilobolo* negotiations) to *umgcagco* (the wedding), things are done for the whole family and not solely for the couple. Hence, you might hear the groom saying, '*ngivusa umuzi kababa*' (I am rebuilding my father's household) or '*ngifuna umuntu ozophekela umama*' (I want someone who will cook for my mother). The slaughtering of the goat to report the arrival of the bride is a sign that she is part of the family from then onwards.

Levirate and sororate marriages

In Africa, there are both levirate and sororate marriage practices after the death of a spouse. They are valued and perceived to be important in continuing the family line in the case of levirate marriage and continuing family ties with the in-laws in the case of sororate marriages.

Levirate marriage (ukungena)

In African communities, including Zulu communities, death does not constitute an end to a marriage. The paying of *ilobolo* and the slaughtering of the goat to accept the wife into the family is an eternal binding bond between the surviving spouse and the in-law family. When a husband dies, his brother must take over all his wives and bear the responsibilities of a husband, taking care of his late brother's wives and children. *Ukungena* is when the man moves into his late brother's house and becomes a husband to the widows. When the husband dies and an approved relative of his lives with the widow and the children, he begets more children for the dead man. This is the leviratic family. The new husband does not pay *ilobolo*. For a Zulu woman, marriage is a long, drawn-out process, whereby she is detached from her native *umndeni* (family) and incorporated gradually into the family of her husband

(Krige and Comaroff 1981: 4). Geoffrey Parrinder (1954: 97) indicates that marriage in Africa is a social affair, concerned as much with the contracting families as with the man and wife.

Sororate marriage (ukuvus' amabele)
When a wife dies, her husband can marry his late wife's younger sister to take care of the children. It is believed that the children's aunt treats them better than a total stranger would, if the man married again on his own without the intervention of the family. Mbiti (1969: 141) mentions:

> Fewer societies have sororate marriages, i.e. when a wife dies the husband marries one of her sisters . . . The 'sister' in this case must be understood in the wider usage of that term, within the kinship system. If the wife does not bear children, it is occasionally arranged that the husband takes her sister to be his wife whether or not the first is dead. In still fewer societies, two sisters are married to the same man. These are other meanings and practices of sororate marriages.

The status of wives in Zulu culture

In my observations at the research site, the status of the wives differs greatly, depending on the order in which they are married. If the woman is the first wife, she knows that she is the most important wife and should her husband die, their firstborn son will be the heir. She knows that she is superior to the other wives. In earlier times, this did not cause as many problems as it does now. The women always submitted to their husbands without question; they were more concerned with pleasing their husband than being happy themselves. However, the superior status of first wives sometimes went to their heads and they would abuse their power and look down upon the subsequent wives. This caused problems within the family and disturbed the social order. Krige (1950: 40) states:

> It seldom, however, happens that the *inGqadi* [right side of kraal ruled by the substitute Great Wife] side inherits, because if the *inkosikazi* [first wife] fails to give birth to the male, the husband usually remedies the deficiency by taking a new wife with the

cattle belonging to the *indlunkulu* [main] hut. This new wife then becomes the subordinate wife to the *indlunkulu* side. She will be placed in the chief hut until she has borne a son, when she is given some other hut in the *indlunkulu* section of the kraal. Her own son is looked upon as the actual son of the chief wife.

C.T. Msimang (1991: 29) makes the point:

> *Kumnandi ukuba iNkosikazi nokuba inqadi nokuba umakoti waseNdlunkulu, okubi ukuba yikhohlo lokhu lona kalidli lutho lomnumzane ngaphandle kokwendlu yalo.*
> It is nice to be the chief wife, and to be the second chief wife (third wife), and to be the wife of *indlunkulu*; what is bad is to be the second wife because she gets nothing from her husband's inheritance, except for what she already has when he dies.

The inequality with regard to the wives' status is another factor that contributes to conflict within polygynous families.

The importance of having a son
In most cases, barrenness in African societies is regarded as the woman's fault. If no children come of the marriage, the man must take another wife. If none of these women give birth to a son, the husband will keep on taking more wives until he finds one who does. Mbiti (1970: 143) records:

> In African societies, the birth of a child is a process which begins long before the child's arrival in this world and continues long thereafter. It is not just a single event which can be recorded on a particular date. Nature brings the child to the world, but society creates the child into a social being, a corporate person . . . Children are buds of the society, and every birth is the arrival of 'spring' when life shoots out and the community thrives. The birth of a child is, therefore, the concern not only of the parents but of many relatives including the living and the departed.

Msimang (1991: 27) further indicates:

> *Naye umnumzane wethembele kakhulu emadodaneni akhe. Uma enecala nomakhelwane, uliqula namadodana akhe, abe izindlebe zakhe. Kanjalo nezikweletu zakhe zaziwa yiwo. Uma ezokwenza umsebenzi phakathi kwekhaya ubikela wona kuqala engakasitsheli isithembu.*
>
> The head of the homestead himself is dependant on his sons. When he has a dispute with the neighbours, he sorts it out with his sons, as they are his ears. Even his debts are known by them. When he is going to do a ritual at home, he informs them first, before telling his wives.

What Msimang is saying is a reflection of what takes place in Zulu society, particularly in my research area. Having a son gives a man a voice in society. He earns respect because of his sons. His sons are superior to his wives and he takes their advice seriously. Mbiti (1969: 25) has this to say about African marriages and the importance of having children:

> If a man has no children or only daughters, he finds another wife so that through her, children (or sons) may be born who would survive him and keep him (with the other living-dead of the family) in personal immortality. Procreation is the absolute way of ensuring that a person is not cut off from personal immortality.

Zulu people believe that if a man dies without a son, the history of the family will vanish because the daughters will get married, leave their father's homestead and change their surnames. The implication is that when a man dies, if he only has daughters, he will leave no family history. This becomes a problem, especially for the wives who have no sons. They feel left out and not as important as those wives who have sons. For this reason, there is usually jealousy and feelings of resentment among the wives.

Research methodology

Thoughout this book, I have used the information obtained from my informants during fieldwork. I had two research assistants, both of which are members of families I interviewed. They were given questionnaires with a list of questions relevant to the research and we then discussed our different tasks. This worked well since everybody knew what they were supposed to do and it gave direction and purpose to the research.

I used a qualitative approach to the research, which involved being in contact with the participants in their natural setting to answer questions related to how they make sense of their lives. Peter Sanders (1975: 45) notes that qualitative researchers may observe the participants and conduct formal and informal interviews to further an understanding of what is going on in the setting from the point of view of those involved in the study. Ethnographic research shares these qualitative traits, but ethnographers more specifically seek understanding of what participants do to create the culture in which they live, and how the culture develops over time.

Interviews

The names I collected during my fieldwork were from the Ngidi clan of KwaMambulu, Kranskop, under Chief Khomba Ngubane. On my initial visit to the research area I was warmly welcomed by the people who knew my parents well. I explained to them the reasons for my visit and that I wanted to explore daily routines from an ethnographic point of view. I wanted to meet them and to collect personal names and write them down, so that everybody could read about them and know of the wonderful place they live in. The people were impressed, possibly because I came from '*eNyuvesi*' (university). I moved from one homestead to the next and was helped by one of my research assistants, who happened to be my cousin. Interviews were conducted in 30 main homesteads. Each homestead might have had three or more smaller homesteads belonging to sons, meaning that up to 100 homesteads were interviewed. I collected about 300 names.

In my interviews, questionnaires were used for the younger generation, but this did not help since many of them did not have enough information. I could not use the questionnaires with the older people because most of them could neither read nor write. Interviews worked well because they provided an opportunity to ask follow-up questions where necessary.

Sanders (1975: 47) notes that ethnography as a method of research forces the researcher to enter the world of the people being investigated. It involves the people under research asking their own questions and structuring their own answers. In this way, answers are not manipulated by the prepared formal questions. The environment in which research is done is as natural as possible and is not threatening to the subjects. Ethnomethodology is a fieldwork method, and fieldwork is about investigating situations and relationships that constitute people's daily lives.

Johann Mouton and H.C. Marais (1988: 1) note that fieldwork is also called 'naturalistic research', which takes place within the natural setting of the social actor. They suggest that qualitative researchers prefer to use unstructured or informal interviews, which employ a set of themes and topics in order to form questions in the course of conversation.

According to Neil Agnew and Sandra Pyke, ethnomethodology is 'a go-and-see' method, the 'eyeball' technique, which is the core of the fieldwork method. They further argue that 'the essence of this science sieve is the observation, description and interpretation of events as they occur in nature or naturally . . . This method requires no manipulation, no controlled experimentation, but rather, the careful observation of episodes as they take place in their usual surroundings' (1982: 45).

Information was verified by cross-checking the responses with other interviewees. The exercise was aimed at 'understanding', rather than 'explanation', as W.J. Schurink (1988: 137) says about the researchers who make use of unstructured interviewing. They are concerned with naturalistic observation, rather than controlled measurement and with the subjective exploration of reality from the perspective of an insider as opposed to the outsider perspective that predominates in the qualitative approach.

The advantage of this method is the construction of reality from the perspective of the insider. It also allows the exploration of other avenues of research that emerge from the conversation. Another advantage is that the insider brings forward questions and insights that might not be captured by a structured interview.

The disadvantages of this method are that it can be time-consuming and the researcher may collect vast amounts of data that are not relevant to their subject. This makes the ordering of facts tedious and makes interpretation difficult. This method requires that, in many cases, the interviewer behaves as an 'insider' in order to capture the cultural and linguistic nuances. Schurink (1988: 140) states that in unstructured interviews, the interviewer limits their own contribution to an absolute minimum. Their role is to introduce the general theme on which information is required, motivate the subjects to participate spontaneously, stimulate them through probing and steer them back tactfully to the research topic when they digress.

Our interviews were often conversations with no time frame. At first it was thought that an hour at each homestead would be sufficient, but three to four hours were frequently spent with one person. It was worth it: the conversations were always interesting and the stories fascinating. Michael H. Agar (1980: 90) proposes that one use what he calls 'Whyte's typology' of informality. This method is ethnographical in the sense that it allows spontaneity and meaningful participation by the researcher, as well as the interviewee. He further suggests that the researcher needs to encourage the informant to keep talking, by word or gesture. Next comes a simple reflection back of the informant's last statement. Then the researcher asks specific questions about that statement, inviting elaboration in a specific direction. So it continues, through the probes on earlier material, until the interviewer requests a change in topic.

Using this method, interviews are conducted much like a natural conversation. Martyn Hammersley and Paul Atkinson make a distinction between ethnographers and survey interviewers:

> The main difference between the way in which ethnographers and survey interviewers ask questions is not, as is sometimes suggested, that one form of interview is 'structured' and the other 'unstructured'. All interviews, like any other kind of social interaction, are structured by both the researcher and the informant. The important distinction is made between standardized and reflective interviewing (1983: 112–13).

They further argue that ethnographers do not decide beforehand the questions they want to ask, though they may enter the interview with a list of issues to be covered. Nor do ethnographers restrict themselves to a single mode of questioning. On different occasions, or at different points in the same interview, my approach could have been non-directive or directive, depending on the function that the questioning was intended to serve. In my case, my approach was mostly non-directive. The only time I referred to my list of questions was between interviews.

The participant observation research method

I drew from the method proposed by Agnew and Pyke (1982: 49). They suggest that participant observers are researchers who are directly involved in the sociocultural life and activities of the group or community within which the investigation is undertaken. While social activities are occurring with researchers taking part, the researchers gain first-hand experience of participating in the life of the community they are researching. Simultaneously, the researchers strive in their observations to be as objective as possible. Agnew and Pyke (1982) suggest: 'The researchers try not to make value judgements like "good" or "bad", "right" or "wrong", "beautiful" or "ugly".'

They also warn the researcher against misleading opinions, beliefs or attitudes about a particular community. They suggest that the ethnographer must participate in people's daily lives for an extended period, watching what happens, listening to what is said, asking questions and collecting available data to throw light on the issues with which they are concerned.

There are different views on the method of participant observation. The view proposed by Hammersley and Atkinson (1983: 97–8) is supported by I.M. Lewis (1976: 24–6). According to Lewis, participant observers must immerse themselves in the community under study and must know their language. Douglas Dziva (1997: 224) is concerned about the depth of intrusion that researchers make in communities they are investigating. He is also concerned with their keeping a critical distance but also acting together with the communities in all that they do. Lewis (1976: 24) advises that researchers must follow events going on around them and must record with accuracy and subtlety. The recording must not disturb the flow and volunteering of information.

The rationale behind this book is a critical examination of names given to children within polygynous families. As an insider, my general observation is that many polygynous homesteads function better than expected because these names act as channels through which people can voice their own opinions freely and without fear of confrontation, which can lead to angering the living-dead.

Life histories

William Labov defines narrative as 'one method of recapitulating past experiences by matching a verbal sequence of clauses to the sequence of events which (it is inferred) actually occurred' (cited in Franzosi 1998: 519). A narrative interview can serve multiple purposes. Firstly, it can refer to a specific episode or experience significant to the storyteller, which leads to a short story. Secondly, the narrative may concern the interviewee's life story from their perspective, which becomes a life history. Thirdly, through the oral history of the interview, where the story develops to also cover communal history, the interviewee can be regarded as an informant (Brinkmann and Kvale 2009). Life stories are often accounts of how an individual enters a group and becomes socialised into it. Life histories emphasise the experience of the individual – how the person copes with society, rather than how society copes with the stream of individuals (Marshall and Rossman 2011: 151). Life histories assist in clarifying cultural changes that have occurred over time. They also capture the way cultural patterns evolve and are linked to the life of an individual (Mkhize 2015: 56). According to Catherine Marshall and Gretchen Rossman, the strength of a life history

> pictures a substantial portion of a person's life; the reader can enter fully into these experiences. Another is that it provides a fertile source of intriguing research questions that may be generative for focusing subsequent studies. And yet the third strength is that life histories depict actions and perspectives across a social group that may be analysed for comparative study. This kind of research requires sensitivity, caring and empathy on the part of the researcher for the researched (2011: 152).

My research took a multidisciplinary approach between names, polygyny and gender politics. I chose to utilise the post-positivistic world view because it challenges the traditional notion of the absolute truth of knowledge and recognises that as humans we cannot be 'positive' about our claims of knowledge when studying the behaviour and actions of humans (Creswell 2009: 6).

Challenges in the interviewing process

One of the challenges faced was the fact that in KwaMambulu a woman wearing trousers is unheard of, so I had to change my dress code and dress like a traditional woman. Secondly, most families wanted me to stay longer at their homes, but I already ended up staying longer in each one than I had anticipated and had to observe a time limit. Thirdly, the stories behind the names were sometimes too long and complicated for my comprehension and I had to ask many questions in order to understand them. Lastly, the language they use is full of *ukuhlonipha* terms (words used in place of certain names and other words that sound like these names to show respect to the in-laws), so in addition to the crash course in the *hlonipha* vocabulary I took from my grandmother, I had to ask my assistants to teach me some words on our way to the next homestead.

2

Polygyny, Gender and Power in Traditional Societies

'Culture' is often used to justify a man taking many wives, regardless of his economic status (Maillu 1988). Many scholars have made the connection between polygyny and contemporary male promiscuity. Polygyny creates an expectation of multiple sexual partners for men and there is a tendency to romanticise African tradition by insisting that in the past polygyny successfully contained male urges (Delius and Glaser 2004). Others argue that polygyny is a result of primal instinct, but is reinforced by social constructs, such as tradition and religion (Hlophe and Ngcaweni 2010). However, Pinky Khoabane (2010) argues that polygyny is used to justify men's infidelity. She draws attention to the enforced double standards in that if a woman commits infidelity she is judged and punished, but when a man does the same it is justified in the name of 'culture'. She also says that polygyny is nothing more than 'socially sanctioned' cheating.

In contemporary times, the study of polygyny is associated with power, hegemonic masculinities and gender relations. Patriarchy and polygyny are deeply rooted in African culture. Tsoaledi Daniel Thobejane argues: 'Polygyny provides men with access to the sexual, reproductive and other services rendered by several women, while wives in polygynous marriages have to share the material and emotional benefits provided by a single man' (2014: 1065). Polygyny thus creates inequality among co-wives since the husband cannot care for and cater to the needs of more than one wife (Dangor 2001). The most important factor of gender relations within polygynous families is that 'to most women it implies unequal relations between men and women, as reflected in men's ability to take several wives versus women's one husband' (Zeitzen 2008: 125).

Inequitable treatment of co-wives causes quarrels within the homestead. This usually happens because the chief wife has special privileges that the younger wives do not have and because of the arrival of a new wife, which often disrupts peaceful and harmonious living. Polygynous set-ups usually affect children born into such marriages because of the rivalry between co-wives. In KwaMambulu the women participants are not aware of their rights or feminism. They use names as weapons of attack and defence. Women cannot voice their opinions freely within the homestead as this might anger the living-dead, so they use names as a defence mechanism against any accusation thrown at them.

In this traditional community, widow inheritance is still prevalent despite the HIV and AIDS pandemic ravaging the community. The widow is expected to bear children for her new husband; culturally, however, the children belong to the deceased husband. These widows are 'inherited' by men who are already married, which further perpetuates polygyny. In this community, polygyny is 'not only flourishing, but constantly changing as well, adapting to ever-changing circumstances and new interpersonal relations' (Zeitzen 2008: 18).

In most traditional societies, polygyny is allowed only through cultural channels such as widow inheritance, barrenness of the chief's wife and post-partum sex taboos. This plays women against themselves and against each other; it becomes their fault that they cannot have children or that they have just had children and therefore cannot have sex or even sleep in the same bed as their husband. This seclusion period can take up to six months, depending on the family and the community rules.

In her research, Leli Nurohmah (2003) discovered in her interviews that nine out of ten women in polygynous marriages had suffered abuse. Women remain under the authority of the men in their lives because 'before marriage, a woman did not have an independent identity. A woman was regarded as the daughter of her father. After marriage she became the wife of her husband' (Kanyoro 2002: 112).

Polygyny is often motivated by economic factors. Supporters of polygyny claim it makes an 'economically stronger family because there are more people working and bringing money into the family' (Thobejane 2014: 1062).

Polygyny in gerontocratic systems

In rural communities women are subjugated within traditional families. Respect for the elders is an unquestioned aspect of traditional societies, which are thus referred to as gerontocratic. The practice of polygyny – for men – confers political and social power, which serves as a mark of prestige (Zeitzen 2008). In traditional societies, having more wives confirms a man's prestige and elevates his status in the society.

Co-wives' relationships with each other determine the kind of life they live within the homestead. Some women are less opposed to polygyny if it is sororal (sisters share a husband), but there is usually competition between co-wives. They compete for their husband's affection, attention, love and economic resources. Catrien Notermans found competition was common in her research district:

> Instead of helping each other with domestic tasks – as the local normative discourse prescribes – co-wives frequently fight for the money and the sexual favours of their husband. The unequal division of money causes sharp arguments and competition between the co-wives, since these women do the agricultural work and almost totally depend on their husbands for money (in Zeitzen 2008: 32).

Polygyny clearly marks power relations in societies. Older men have power over women and younger men as they control the lifestyle and decisions within the homestead. Gerontocracy always perceives women as children, to be taken care of and controlled. This system also encourages older men to take much younger wives. The age difference, together with the prestige, power and status, renders gender equity impossible (Crosby 1937). In rural societies, 'there is a general tendency for the number of wives to increase with the age as well as the power and prestige of each elder' (Zeitzen 2008: 52). Husbands then control wives by labelling them as mere sexual partners and bearers of children. Bearing children is an essential component of a polygynous marriage for women who want to have a claim on their husband's estate. Co-wives compete on having more children, particularly male children.

Gender and power relations within polygynous families

R.W. Connell developed a theory of gender and power as a 'social structural theory based on existing philosophical writings of sexual inequality and gender and power imbalance. According to the theory of gender and power, there are three major social structures that characterise the gendered relationships between men and women: the sexual division of labour, the sexual division of power, and the cathexis' (1987: 54).

Gender and power are deeply rooted in family systems and societal structures (Goodrich et al. 1988). For Zulu people, family is a collective structure of the extended family and the community. Women's gender is a major factor in human rights violations around the world, which emphasises that women have limited control over their lives and the decisions they take (Earth and Sthapit 2002; Russo and Smith 2006).

Polygyny is deeply embedded in gender relations. In polygynous societies the husband never has to go without sex or somebody to take care of him. The wives' sexual needs are not considered important, be it in the post-partum stage or during menstruation. In these situations the woman is simply ignored and given attention only when her husband 'needs' her. It has been argued by many scholars and feminists that polygyny exacerbates the sexual exploitation of women. Co-wives are not allowed to have extramarital affairs and the husband makes sure that his wives' fidelity is guaranteed. Polygynous men are commended for having multiple partners, whereas women who do the same are labelled as promiscuous, shunned and called names. The husband's economic prowess is important in securing more wives and for him to have power over them.

Polygyny automatically negates women's empowerment because it enforces male dominance and suppresses the female voice. A study conducted in Ghana demonstrated that women and their domestic roles are perceived as replaceable at any time. It also revealed that there are gender inequalities with regard to reproduction and family planning within polygynous families (Agadjanian and Ezeh 2000). A wife's worth and autonomy are determined by several factors, which include, but are not limited to, her position in the family hierarchy, what her husband considers important about her and whether she has her own space (a separate household). Co-wives are compelled to co-operate with each other because it is believed to eradicate competition, and jealousies are reduced through the sharing of domestic responsibilities.

Polygyny and gender relations

The term 'gender relations' refers to the relationships arising from the perceived differences between men and women based on their reproductive differences (Connell and Messerschmidt 2005). Polygynous set-ups, by their very nature, 'reinforce hegemonic notions of gender based on cultural and religious traditions' (Mkhize 2015: 4). There is a vast body of literature on polygyny and its effects on women and children (see, for example, Oyefeso and Adegoke 1992; Madhavan 2002; Tabi, Doster and Cheney 2010). A study conducted by Mustafa Ozkan and colleagues demonstrates that the most common reasons for accepting polygynous marriages were 'cultural obligations; infertility; not giving birth to a son; medical illness; and the husband having had an affair with the junior wife before he married her' (Ozkan et al. 2006: 218).

In developing societies, where women have been emancipated through education and economic opportunities, this practice is becoming less favourable (Zeitzen 2008). This is testimony to the fact that 'tradition is fluid; its content is redefined by each generation, and its timelessness may be situationally constructed' (Linnekin 1983: 242). Obonye Jonas (2012) argues that a decision to get married is taken in the context of the value system prevailing in that particular society. The claim by patriarchs that co-wives consent to their husband taking more wives is thus false, since women have no say in a patriarchal society (Jonas 2012: 147).

Few studies have examined anthroponyms in polygynous families from the perspective of gender relations. Most research explores polygyny from an anthropological perspective. Many scholars have written on the impact of polygyny on women (see, for example, Al-Krenawi 1999; Elbedour et al. 2002). Polygyny is largely criticised by Western feminists, whereas African feminists and womanists are divided. There are those who argue that it is part of the culture and therefore should be preserved, while others are against the practice. In the course of my research, I observed that the effects of polygyny include jealousy and constant fighting among the co-wives. Anthroponyms are bestowed so that they can diffuse the situation and air pent-up emotions caused by competition and fighting among the co-wives.

Gender relations in an African cultural context

Culture plays an important role in interfacing with the psychodynamics of gender identity (Diamond 2006: 1104). Zamambo Mkhize asserts that 'male power also allows the development of social and interpersonal definitions that devalue women and femininity and strengthen and legitimise the gender system' (2015: 33). This correlation between culture and gender results in a disproportional division of household duties, founded on the assumption that women derive pleasure and fulfilment only from home, husband and children (Lui 2013: 2).

Gender has become an important phenomenon in recent times (Nencel 2007) because it gives meaning to the social and cultural mores of masculinity and femininity. Gender should be viewed as a social and socio-cultural construct because it exists within culture-specific realities: 'As gender is a construction, the meaning given to masculinity and femininity is related to culture-specific common-sense and existing social structures in a society, and therefore strongly connected to time and place' (Poelma and Stuijt 2015: 16).

Polygyny and modernity

Polygyny was discouraged by both colonialists and Christian missionaries in Africa. However, since this injunction came with no sanctions, it could not be eliminated (Zeitzen 2008). As Gibson Kamau Kuria points out: 'Colonial governments in Africa typically wrote its gradual abandonment into their charters. The main problem was how to integrate polygyny into a marriage and family law code that was based on Western monogamous marriage and had no foundations in an African context' (1987: 289). Colonial powers and missionaries tried unsuccessfully to eradicate polygyny in sub-Saharan countries when they attempted to replace polygyny through changing marriage regulations and giving preferential treatment to monogamous men (Ngondo a Pitshandenge 1994). Colonial governments enacted policies and laws that interfered with traditional social structures. Among their new laws were *imali yekhanda* (head taxes, which all black men had to pay to white authorities) and *ilobolo* was set very high for ordinary men to afford in another attempt to curb men from taking more wives. This in turn created another challenge as men began taking concubines as a justifiable alternative. In Ghana in 1974, Christine Oppong found that 'men are allowed, and even expected, to be involved with more than one woman, and can only be accused of adultery if they are involved with a married woman' (Oppong 1974: 98).

Cohabitation is considered the new form of urban African polygyny and is also to the man's advantage. Polygyny has not gone away; it has simply changed form. This, modern women argue, gives power to men who are perceived as being in charge of their fate. Men enjoy conjugal benefits without the pressure and responsibilities that come with marriage and women are free of the expectations of the husband and the in-laws that they will perform certain duties. Many women who get involved with men who are already married are opposed to the institution of marriage. They view marriage as an oppressive structure meant only for the benefit of men. Since divorce is shunned in traditional societies, these women feel that being girlfriends gives them an opportunity to stay or leave the relationship without having to explain their choices to anyone. In many African societies, marriages are fluid and can no longer be rigidly located within cultural and/or religious contexts.

However, in many rural areas in sub-Saharan Africa, polygyny exists under a gerontocracy and a strong belief in the living-dead and the powers they are believed to possess (Caldwell, Reddy and Caldwell 1987). The aim of polygyny is to benefit the husband and his family, to support agriculture and to produce many children who will carry on the family name. In traditional societies such as KwaMambulu, when a man marries a new wife, he clears a field for her and her children to plough (Boserup 1985). Women in sub-Saharan countries also have a much lower status than men. This becomes magnified when they are childless and spouseless in a context where women are treated as a form of property (Boserup 1970). It has been claimed that *ilobolo* is paid as an exchange for the labour provided by the wife and her capacity to produce children (Hayase and Liaw 1997).

Polygyny and poverty

In KwaMambulu, most families live below the poverty line. The husbands struggle to provide for the whole family. When girls reach marriageable age, they are married off so that their brothers can use the cows (and/or money) to pay *ilobolo*. This indirectly controls the time that these girls enter into marriage. In most cases they get married in their teens, which means they drop out of school to become wives and fall pregnant quickly. Thus, they grapple with parenthood while they are still children themselves, without the support of their husbands who usually work in distant towns and come home a couple of times a year. This arrangement leads to poverty, as the husbands themselves are school drop-outs without professional careers. The polygynous arrangement means more children are born into the family with not enough resources for them to live the same lives as their peers, which perpetuates poverty and suffering within families.

Many scholars highlight the effects of polygyny on the well-being of the family, the household economy and resource allocation (Boserup 1970; Ezeh 1997; Brown 1981; Grossbard 1993). Michèle Tertilt (2005) argues that polygyny may be a contributing factor to under-development in sub-Saharan Africa as a result of men investing in wives, rather than in physical property. It is also claimed that men tend to be in polygamous unions to the detriment of women's livelihoods (Jacoby 1995). Natasha Wagner and Mathias Rieger (2011) provide evidence that polygamy affects the children negatively and they propose that this may be the reason Africa's economy is suffering. Eric D. Gould, Omer Moav and Avi Simhon (2008) propose a model that predicts the education of women will lead to a decline in polygamy and that will in turn produce educated children. In Côte d'Ivoire the children of junior wives had worse health issues because of neglect by their fathers (Strauss and Mehra 1990). In addition, plural marriages affect children's health and schooling as the children of senior wives receive a better education (Mammen 2009). The rivalry between co-wives can also disrupt the life within the household (Kazianga and Klonner 2009). From the literature consulted, it is clear that plural marriage disrupts the peace in the homestead as husbands may prefer one wife over the other. This causes rivalry between co-wives and disadvantages the children of the less-favoured wives.

Hegemonic masculinity and polygyny

The concept of hegemonic masculinity was formulated by Australian sociologist R.W. Connell (1987). It generally refers to dominant 'acceptability norms' of male behaviour from a gender perspective (Blackbeard and Lindegger 2007) and is used to justify men being in a position of domination over women. It is a representation of society's ideal of how male behaviour should be. Hegemonic masculinity can be used to describe 'conventional and stereotypic' forms of masculinity (Davies and Eagle 2013: 66).

According to Connell, masculinity is 'simultaneously a place in gender relations, the practices through which men and women engage that place in gender, and the effects of these practices on bodily experience, personality and culture' (1995: 17). Connell is of the opinion that gender hegemony is perpetuated through subordination and marginalisation of women, and the marginalisation of other masculinities. Hegemonic masculinity is perceived as 'the configuration of gender practice which embodies the currently accepted answer to the problem of the legitimacy of patriarchy, which guarantees (or is taken to guarantee) the dominant position of men and the subordination of women' (Connell 1995: 77).

One form of femininity is defined around compliance with this subordination and is oriented to accommodate the interests and desires of men: 'The concept of "emphasised femininity" focuses on compliance to patriarchy, and this is still highly relevant in contemporary mass culture' (Connell and Messerschmidt 2005: 848). Other forms of femininity are defined centrally by strategies of resistance or forms of non-compliance or by complex strategic combinations of compliance, resistance and co-operation. In Connell's theory, subordination is a mechanism for the ascendancy of hegemonic masculinity. In applying Connell's framework to femininity, Karen D. Pyke and Denise L. Johnson (2003) identify a relationship between subordination and domination in white and Asian femininity.

Harry Brod (1987) argues that pervasive images of masculinity potrayed in the media suggest that the 'real man' is physically strong, aggressive and in control. However, the structural dichotomy between manual and mental labour means that no one's world fulfils all these conditions. Hegemonic masculinity embodies the most honoured way of being a man and it legitimates the global subordination of women to men (Connell and Messerschmidt 2005). James J. Gray and Rebecca L. Ginsberg argue:

> Women's rise in power has created a crisis in masculinity all over the world. In particular, in cultures in which the traditional male role as bread-winner and protector has declined and in which machine has replaced muscle, the pursuit of muscularity has become one of the few ways left for men to exhibit their masculine selves (2007: 19).

R.W. Connell and James Messerschmidt (2005) and Chris Beasley (2008) posit that hegemonic masculinities can be analysed on three levels. The first level is local, which is constructed in the arena of face-to-face interaction of families and immediate communities, as found in ethnographic and life-history research. The second is regional, which is constructed at the level of the culture or the nation state. The third level is global, which is constructed in transnational arenas such as world politics, transnational business and the media.

Robert Morrell (1994, 1998, 2001) has utilised hegemonic masculinity to explain the form, nature and dynamics of male power. Morrell situates his definition of hegemonic masculinity within the Connell framework as 'the form of masculinity which is dominant in society. This is not a question of head counts, but a "question of relations of cultural domination"' (1994: 607–8). Hegemonic masculinity has culture as its backdrop. Máirtín Mac an Ghaill defines hegemonic masculinity as the ultimate form of oppression:

> In addition to oppressing women, hegemonic masculinity silences or subordinates other masculinities, positioning these in relation to itself such that the values expressed by these other masculinities are not those that have currency or legitimacy. In turn, it presents its own version of masculinity, of how men

should behave and how putative 'real men' do behave, as the cultural ideal (1994: 608).

Robert Morrell, Rachel Jewkes and Graham Lindegger agree and add that 'hegemonic masculinity is synonymous with problematic male attitudes and behaviour, such as violence and abuse of women and children, substance abuse and risky sexual behaviours' (2012: 13).

Women, polygyny and power

Each person's sense of gender is an inextricable melding of personally created and cultural meaning. Nancy Chodorow draws from her own experiences and argues that her conscious construction of gender includes a strong feminism and anger at male privilege and societal sexism. She explains that her feminism is the result of growing up in an ideologically male-dominant family that explicitly valued her brothers over herself and her sisters (Chodorow 1995: 534). Gender is the family's organising principle and gender distinctions are the substratum of hierarchy and oppression within families (Chodorow 1995).

Domestic patriarchy relies on support from society (Connell 1987). In European culture, children are not explicitly taught that women are inferior, whereas Zulu culture implicitly and explicitly promotes the idea that men are superior to women (Mkhize 2011). However, in African societies, power is not so much gender-specific as it is age-specific (Oyewumi 1997). This usually means that women and young men are treated as children by senior men. It is also used to separate gender and sex roles within the family and in the community. This confines women to the home front, which is centred around childcare and domestic chores, while the public sphere is reserved for men: 'In a gendered, male-headed two-parent household, the male is conceived as the breadwinner and the female is associated with home and nurture' (Mkhize 2015: 24). As a result, women's contributions are usually undervalued (26). As research conducted by Andrea Doucet reveals:

> Women have been responsible for the bulk of routine housework and caring for others, while men tend to spend their domestic work time on non-routine domestic work. Women's 'second

shift' of gendered responsibilities indicate that mothers 'felt more responsible for the home'. Only recently men have shown a willingness to spend more time with their children . . . change has been very slow and the proportion of men assuming equal responsibility is currently very small (2015: 224).

Ruth A. Wallace (1991) argues that a gender system of maintenance and reproduction asserts superior male power, which allows men to coerce women into assuming work roles that reinforce their disadvantaged status, at both macro and micro levels. The social constructivist approach argues that gender is formed by social and cultural forces such as prescribed tasks and dress codes, based on perceived differences between men and women.

Gender is not only a cause but also a consequence, instrument and embodiment of power over relations. It is a key mechanism through which power not only constrains, but also constitutes individuals and is perhaps one of the most persistent forms of 'invisible power' in our world. In many contexts, what it means to be a woman is to be powerless; it is considered 'feminine' to be quiet, accommodating and obedient. By contrast, it is considered 'manly' to exercise power, that is, to get others to do what you want them to do.

The patriarch has coercive powers

Coercive power implies that there is an ability to impose penalties for non-compliance (Bass 1990). According to Timothy R. Hinkin and Chester A. Schriesheim (1989), coercive power is the ability to administer and/or remove things that the other person does not desire. Polygynists are more likely to rely on coercive power because it is a result of the authoritarian position they have over their wives. This position is given freely to them through the culture. Greg J. Duncan and Jeanne Brooks-Gunn (1997) conceptualise gender in terms of a hegemonic relationship and found evidence suggesting that those scoring high on authoritarianism were inclined to maintain traditional gender roles and demonstrate a rejection of non-traditional, gender-role identity. O'Neill and Domingo point out:

> Adverse gender norms affect all women – but how they affect them depends on other structural factors . . . In all patriarchal societies, but particularly in extremely conservative societies, women who wish to advance gender equality also need to convince potential male allies, make deals and compromises and frame issues in ways that minimise hard opposition (2015: 5).

Polygyny is sometimes used by men to manipulate women into conforming to their demands. For example, a man may manipulate his wife's fear of his having a younger and more beautiful sister wife. This interferes with women's self-worth and is used to control women's assertive self within a marriage (Ross 2002: 24).

Politics, power and prestige

Polygyny serves a political function in traditional societies and also 'serves as a marker of power' (Zeitzen 2008: 50). Furthermore, 'old members of society achieve their dominant position through control over the means of production as well as reproduction, by controlling access to wives and sexual partners; they typically also control access to symbolic and religious systems, giving them added legitimacy'. For polygynists, this arrangement gives them political influence and power to control their wives. It also gives them a mark of prestige:

> Within polygamous societies, multiple wives are typically status symbols denoting wealth and power for the husband. It signals that he has the resources to build up a large household and maintain it. This places him in an elite group within societies where most men can only afford to establish and maintain a monogamous household (Zeitzen 2008: 53).

The fact that any subsequent marriage starts as an affair gives men the upper hand in sexual relationships. They can easily have it both ways. It takes time before the 'mistress' officially becomes a wife. While the man is 'cheating', his current wife's dignity is not considered and is deeply compromised by his behaviour.

There is also no guarantee that the new relationship is free from sexually transmitted infections, including HIV and AIDS. The risk of infection is prevalent since most women do not go through virginity testing, which is supposedly proof of abstinence before marriage. The first wife will usually suffer because once she is married she must wait for her husband to 'come home' after 'looking for' his potential wife or wives.

Polygyny and women's rights

From time immemorial, polygyny has been embedded in African culture and in the religion of family life. It continues to be the 'most distinctive feature of African marriage' (Garenne and Van de Walle 1989: 267). However, the fight for gender equality has been at the centre of social change since 1945 and 'polygyny . . . and other cultural practices are as legitimately subject to criticism within the context and setting of human rights as is any other structural aspect of society' (Jonas 2012: 142). According to Frantz Fanon (2004: 211), polygyny constitutes an assault on women's rights to equality and it infringes upon women's rights to be free from discrimination (Cook and Kelly 2006: 11). Jonas takes this criticism even further and says: 'Polygamous marriage contravenes a woman's right to equality with men and can have such serious emotional and financial consequences for her and her dependants that such marriages ought to be discouraged and prohibited' (2012: 146). Furthermore, the continued existence of polygyny 'violates fundamental rights such as rights to dignity, equality, health and equal protection under the law. It also exacerbates women's already lower socio-economic status by forcing women to share already scarce resources with co-wives and their children' (148).

Polygyny in mainstream popular culture and television

Three Wives, One Husband is an American documentary series about fundamentalist Mormons living in the Rockland Ranch area on the outskirts of Utah. They choose to live in the desert because they want to practise polygyny (which is part of their religion) in peace. They are still fighting for the legalisation of polygyny.

Abel Morrison's brother dies after a long fight with cancer, leaving behind his two wives and seven children. Jim's dying wish was for

Abel to marry his widows. Abel is sympathetic towards his brother's family, especially to the children who will grow up without a father. But marrying Jim's widows will see him having five wives and nineteen children. Talk of his marrying these two widows has destabilised an already unstable family. At the time of Jim's death, Abel had taken a third wife, who had just given birth. Abel agreed to marry his brother's widows without the consent of his wives. He decided on his own and felt that if any of his wives were unhappy with his decision, they could leave the marriage. His second wife, Beth, already felt neglected with two co-wives married to her husband, so the thought of adding two more wives seemed impossible. Abel's stance was that he took a decision that he felt was right. He would pray to God to soften his wives' hearts, so that they would stand with him on his decision. Beth's concern is that the existing wives would not get enough attention from their husband if additional wives were to join their already unstable family. Another wife, Marina, supports the idea of levirate marriage because she feels that it would be easier for Jim's family to adjust.

Each time Abel takes a selfish unilateral decision, he uses the pronoun 'we', so that his wives feel included. This is his strategy to make them believe that they are somehow part of the decision-making process, when in fact he is the one in charge. The family dynamics of Abel and his three wives were already compromised when he contemplated starting a levirate marriage despite his wives' reservations. He uses their faith to convince them to agree to the addition of two more wives. On the show, the patriarch is the only participant who is at ease with this multiple partnership. When interviewed individually, each wife voices her concerns about this set-up. They point out that they only agreed to it because it 'makes them feel closer to God', as their religion prescribes. As unhappy as the wives are, in the end, they choose to stay with their husband because they believe that it is their godly duty to submit to him and allow polygamy to continue. This, they believe, makes them fight their fleshly desires, alleviate jealousy and be closer to God, the kind of sacrifice that will be rewarded in heaven. Jim's first wife was not keen on marrying Abel, but the second wife wanted to continue being part of her late husband's family and agreed to marry Abel.

Portrayal of polygyny in Sister Wives

Sister Wives is an American reality television series. The husband, Kody, is only legally married to the first wife, Meri. The other three wives are his 'spiritual partners', according to his church and religion. Kody has a strict schedule to adhere to when it comes to visiting each woman's house. He must also plan date nights with each of them. All the women work to contribute to the well-being of the family. Kody had been 'married' to his three wives for some time before Robyn became the fourth addition to the family. She came with three children from her previous marriage. Her joining the family caused much instability. As the new wife she received most of the husband's attention, which upset the other wives. Mormon fundamentalist plural marriages are perceived as high levels of love and sacrifice, a 'more-people-to-love-you-and-to-love-back' scenario. The relationships between the sister wives is difficult. Their belief that polygyny is God's purpose for their lives does not negate their feelings of insecurity and jealousy caused by sharing a husband. The first and second wife had to go through counselling to try to salvage their strained relationship. They both had suppressed anger and hidden resentment towards each other.

By the end of the show, Kody decides to divorce his only legal wife, Meri, so that he can legally marry his fourth wife, Robyn. His reason was that he wanted to legally adopt Robyn's children from her previous marriage, so that they could have medical aid and insurance benefits. This was hurtful to Meri, who, after 24 years of marriage, was so easily replaced by a much younger woman. She took this as a demotion from being a wife to a mere concubine (spiritual partner).

Portrayal of polygyny in uThando Nes'thembu

The South African television series *uThando NeS'thembu* is modelled to a certain extent on its American counterparts. The difference is that in South Africa, polygyny is legal if the first wife is married under customary law. Legally, the wives have an equal claim to the estate of the patriarch, but culturally the first wife has the authority to oversee things and her sister wives have to consult her for any decision regarding the welfare of the household. This show is recorded in a rural area of Umzinto, south of Durban, in KwaZulu-Natal. The patriarch, Musa Mseleku, is traditional and conservative and staunchly believes in African religion. He believes that the wealth he has accumulated results from his obedience to his living-dead and the appeasement rituals he often performs for them. He has given South Africans a window into the practice of polygyny in modern times. Each of his four wives has a beautiful house, a car and a joint budget for monthly groceries. He spends about R25 000 each month for his wives and children. He claims that he loves all his wives equally. This has fuelled conversation around the practice of polygyny, which, until very recently, has been perceived as primitive and unsophisticated.

The show *uThando NeS'thembu* has encouraged many men to come out and express their aspirations to be polygynists. For many African men, polygyny is seen as a practice meant to keep a man happy sexually and to give him higher social status. Mseleku has asserted that the show was meant to refute myths regarding polygyny that are perpetuated by feminists and the mainstream media.

Once women are married, they are no longer addressed by their first names. Their terms of address become *Ma-* (daughter of) prefixed to the maiden name. This demonstrates that even in modern times women are viewed as the property of the men in their families. According to traditionalists, this is seen as a sign of respect, but it can also be argued that it strips women of their identity. They are seen as objects that can be passed from one man to the next. Prior to marriage they are under the authority of their fathers, uncles and/or brothers; when they marry they become the property of their husbands.

MaCele (daughter of Cele)
MaCele is the chief wife. Culturally, her position gives her decisive powers on family matters. The husband must consult her first before he does most things. The other wives know that they must get her approval. She seems content with being the first wife and the powers that come with that. Her co-wives organised an appreciation party for her, at which she pointed out that her position as the first wife will remain unchallenged. She asserted that even if her husband married more wives, she knows that she is the one he loves. This dampened the spirit of the party and left the viewers thinking her arrogant and unappreciative. Throughout

the first season of the series she seemed to be struggling with sharing her husband with his other wives. She even pointed out that when he came into her house she expected him to act like her husband and not like a polygynist. She was informed from the outset (by her husband) that he would be taking more wives. She knowingly married a polygynist, but did not find it easy living in this set-up.

MaYeni (daughter of Yeni)

MaYeni was supposed to have been the chief wife, but her family initially refused to agree to her marriage to the patriarch. By the time her family agreed to the *ilobolo* negotiations, Mseleku had already married his first wife. MaYeni is an introvert and rarely participates in family discussions. She goes with whatever has been decided for her. She is often told what to do by the extroverted MaKhumalo, who assumes the leadership role each time MaCele (the first wife) is away.

MaKhumalo (daughter of Khumalo)

MaKhumalo has no biological children, but is rearing some of her husband's children from previous relationships as if they are her own. In the series she portrays herself as the understanding and submissive wife. She is the one the husband goes to when there is conflict and his wives are fighting for his attention. She goes around the province of KwaZulu-Natal giving talks to women about issues that affect their marriages and polygyny. She emphasises the fact that this kind of a marriage is not for everybody. Her most important assertion is that the man must be in a financially stable position to take care of his wives. She does point out that women should not be in relationships or marry already-married men, because this complicates things. This leaves most of her audiences confused, as she did the exact opposite. However, she does admit that it was a mistake and a sin for her to marry a man who already had two wives.

MaNgwabe (daughter of Ngwabe)

MaNgwabe is the youngest wife and has a child living with a disability. She claims that she agreed to be the fourth wife because she loves her husband. She admits that being in this type of a marriage comes with its own challenges, but has built a strong relationship with her husband.

The patriarch

In *uThando NeS'thembu*, the patriarch calls family meetings when there are issues to be discussed. He listens to the wives' wishes and needs, but the final decision lies with him. He is in control of their financial and social lives. His micro-management style sees him planning family holidays and date nights. He decides on which car to buy for each of his wives. They are obliged to report everything to him, even how much petrol they put in their cars. Most women in these types of marriages are lonely. They are not allowed to have extramarital affairs as that is a benefit only reserved for men.

Polygynous husbands usually use the collective pronoun 'we' when addressing issues that affect the family as a unit. This in some way silences the wives and they end up not talking and/or freely expressing themselves. This is done by men to make women feel as though they are part of the decision-making process. In all three shows, the families feel that they should share their stories so that people in monogamous marriages understand the intracacies of this kind of marriage. The emphasis is on being a family, being friendly and accepting of each other. Co-wives are made to believe that they belong to their husbands, which reinforces their identity within the family. They are aware that they cannot curb their husband's roving eye when it comes to other women, but it is not easy for them to accept.

Love and affection seem to take a back seat in these television series; what comes to the forefront is the portrayal of women as men's objects. They have to answer to his call and must satisfy his needs. In all three cases, the addition of more wives causes instability in the family. Co-wives are not happy with their husbands marrying more wives, but they must suppress their feelings, keep their opinions to themselves and focus on the positive aspects that their marriages provide. In most cases, women focus on the fact that the husband is a responsible person who can financially provide for his family. Their emotional and sexual needs are ignored in these marriages because their lives depend on the schedule the husband has drawn up for them and his availability to visit each wife.

In *uThando NeS'thembu*, the treatment the four wives receive from the patriarch undermines the happily married, blended family life the collective may want to portray. They are treated as children. All decisions are taken for them. As the reality of the show takes on its own life, the pretence sometimes falls away. The viewers witness tempers rising, exchange of nasty words, condescension and the shedding of tears, all in the name of loving the patriarch. His micro-management style is indicative of the patriarchal control that has challenged women from the beginning of time. It leaves the wives having to check their decisions with him, having to account for their spending and asking for permission to go out. The patriarch does not allow them to go to any function where alcohol is served if he is not going to be present. The wives have normalised this kind of treatment and perceive it as part of his male 'authority'. It must be noted that in patriarchal societies, submission is often confused with respect. At all times an adherent wife is preferred to an assertive one. The show set tongues wagging, especially when the patriarch mentioned that he satisfies all his wives sexually, which seems impossible for a busy businessman with four wives. He must adhere to a strict schedule for each of his wives to make sure that there is harmony in his marriages.

Rural women and their duties

Rural women usually do not have the electric appliances their urban counterparts have and so the duties of rural women and young girls include collecting wood – a chore that no man would ever do. As a result, they go to forests, which can take a whole day, depending on how far the forest is from their home. They usually go in groups to keep each other company and to protect each other from harm. These women and children also often have to walk long distances to fetch water. They use steel buckets and plastic containers and from an early age they master the art of carrying these containers on their heads without hand support.

Cooking is the domain of women in Zulu culture. This pattern developed from the socialisation that teaches men at an early age that their mothers and sisters are supposed to cook for them. In KwaMambulu, it is unheard of for a man to cook. If his wife needs to go somewhere, she makes sure that she cooks first. Men who cook for their wives are seen as weak and as having been affected by love potions used to make them submit to their wives.

Cleaning the household is also the domain of women. These rural women use different ways of cleaning their houses, such as using cow dung to polish the floors. They have no sophisticated machinery, although there are a few that have linoleum on their floors, and who use cleaning detergents.

Child-rearing is the responsibility of women. It should be remembered that in rural communities, no woman can choose not to have children as they can in more urban communities. African women have also mastered the art of carrying their children on their backs. They can do many chores, like collecting wood, fetching water and cleaning their houses, with children on their backs. In addition, rural women must take care of their mothers-in-law. Unlike their urban counterparts, who can send the elderly to old-age homes, rural women take it upon themselves to care for their elders.

'Witchcraft' in African societies and its gender implications

As Hazel Rose Markus and Shinobu Kitayama note: 'Knowing and understanding people in other cultures, from their own perspectives, is increasingly important if we are to be effective participants in this world' (1994: 346). The idea of witchcraft is central to the day-to-day experiences of African people and it permeates many aspects of life in sub-Saharan Africa. There is constant awareness of the reality of evil induced by witchcraft:

> Most Africans believe that witchcraft causes unusual phenomenon like accidents, conflicts, death, domestic and public aggression, loss of poverty, sickness and failure. The mystical powers are controlled by witches who possess powers which stop or influence the aforementioned phenomena . . .
>
> Mystical power is known or experienced by nearly all Africans who have grown up in a traditional environment. They will have witnessed magic, divination, witchcraft or other mysterious phenomena (Nyabwari and Kagema 2014: 9).

Laurenti Magesa (1997) holds that witchcraft has a central place in the moral structure of African religion. Witchcraft is considered an enemy of life as it is against harmony, good order, neighbourliness and virtuous company. As Bernard Gechiko Nyabwari and Dickson Nkonge Kagema maintain:

> Witchcraft is against all that holds the community together – the solidarity and the unity of society, the fine balance between the living and the dead, order and survival in the universe. Witches are people who cannot control their impulses, who have insatiable desires and hatreds, are often unsociable, selfish or arrogant (2014: 13).

Belief in the practice of witchcraft is deeply rooted in the minds of Zulu people. There is always a need to explain ailments and bad luck. When a person falls ill it is usually suspected that it is the use of witchcraft by extended family members. Usually the family will consult an *isangoma* (diviner) or *inyanga* (herbalist) to ascertain the cause of illness.

Condemnation and sweeping generalisations, rather than respect and understanding, have become the norm in the West's approach to African beliefs and practices (Ter Haar 2007). 'Witchcraft', a European word, is applied to African practices. African people have often tried to align themselves linguistically with dominant economic powers and Jim Harries argues that African people 'echo ideas from the West in order to avoid being ridiculed. Historical and spiritual/religious circumstances that propelled wealth creation in the West are downplayed among Africans' (2010: 139). Barry Hallen and J. Olubi Sodipo analyse why it is not possible to explain African witchcraft in Western terms:

> There is no reason to assume that witchcraft in Africa is the same as was witchcraft in Europe, anymore than there was reason to assume that the English-language concept 'witchcraft' may serve as an accurate translation of its supposed African-language equivalents. Whatever is translated as being 'witchcraft' in Africa (or even in one place in Africa) may well be a very different thing from whatever it is elsewhere in the world and history (1986: 69).

The word 'witchcraft' is sometimes incorrectly used to refer to *izinyanga* (herbalists) and *izangoma* (diviners). The inadequacy of the word 'witchcraft' (*ubuthakathi* in isiZulu) is that it may be used to refer to any unscientific use of *imithi* in English. However, in isiZulu it only refers to the misuse of *imithi* by sorcerers or witches (*abathakathi*).

Witchcraft as a gendered phenomenon

In most traditional societies, it is usually the women who are suspected of practising witchcraft. The practice of witchcraft as an evil phenomenon therefore has gender as its focal point. South African witch-hunts have seen many women killed, ostracised and banned from their villages. Talking about how witchcraft is viewed in African communities, John Mbiti states:

> Generally, Africans regard witchcraft as the supposed power of a person to harm others by occult or supernatural means. To this day, witchcraft is not tolerated in African communities. People suspected of practicing witchcraft face dire consequences. In some communities they get banished from their homes, their homes are burnt down, they get shot, stabbed or strangled (1969: 192).

Suspicion of the practice of witchcraft is enough for a woman to be persecuted. These occurrences expose the misogynistic nature of traditional and patriarchal societies. In KwaMambulu, women suspect other women (co-wives) of witchcraft because of jealousy. Some of these suspicions and accusations are merely distractions aimed at obtaining sympathy from the husband so that the accusing wife can get more attention. Some suspicions develop from the recurrence of infant mortality and stillborn children. As Harries shows:

> Barren women are assumed to wish for the death of their co-wife's children rather than to sit in lonely misery as another woman enjoys the company of devoted offspring. Jealousy, it is believed, surely troubles old widows who observe other women enjoying their husband's company and wealth. More likely to be

neglected and ignored than men when sickly or aged, old women are prone to bitterness and jealousy (2010: 142).

Belief in jealousy-induced witchcraft is very strong among Africans. Some people are said to be preoccupied with trying to bring down those who seem to be doing better than they are, while potential victims avoid the appearance of doing well in order not to stir the jealousy of witches (Harries 2010: 143). These 'witches' are not members of a particular cult (as is the case in Euro-Western or West African contexts), but they function on an individual need-to-act basis.

Overcoming witchcraft in Africa

The belief in and practice of witchcraft is viewed by some as superstitious, barbaric and unnecessary in the twenty-first century. It is felt by some that since witchcraft cannot be explained scientifically, it is irrelevant and should not be taken seriously. For some, education is the solution (Dovlo 2007); some advocate Christianity and the church as the solution (Kgatla 2007). However, Elias K. Bongmba (2007) warns that the church sometimes enhances the belief in witchcraft. The feeling is that it is difficult for people to completely suppress their beliefs:

> Changing witchcraft beliefs in Africa, then, can only be the result of a long-term process. What is needed . . . is to cultivate alternative modes of interpretation of life-events in order eventually to undermine the witchcraft mentality. But any type of education in this regard . . . must be culturally based in order to be effective (Ter Haar 2007: 24–5).

3

Veneration of the Living-Dead and Zulu Anthroponymy

Alexander Jebadu (2006: 4) states that the religious focus of ancestral practices is based on the universal belief in the continuation of life after corporeal death, in the existence of the Absolute Being as the only source of life, both for the living and the dead, and in the continuous communion between the living community in the world and the living-dead in the great beyond.

Scholars such as Lenard Nyirongo (1997: 87) and Allan Anderson (1991: 81) have argued that the term 'veneration' is preferable to 'worship' on the grounds that there is no evidence of an apotheosis of the ancestors. My research affirms this view. Goodman Agrippa Khathide (2003: 314) maintains that although the notion that ancestral rituals are to be considered in the context of their social significance and therefore as a form of veneration, rather than worship, there are some unresolved issues. He argues that Johannes Triebel's assertion that the ancestors are venerated does not consider that the ancestors are feared (2002: 192). My research concurs with Y.C. Ro's assertion that the term 'ancestor cult' is not an appropriate term to use in this context, mainly because of the pejorative connotations attached to the term (1988: 7).

The primary reason for ancestral veneration in the African context is not to seek a communication with the dead by magically conjuring up the souls of the dead to obtain information from them about the revelation of unknown causes or about the future course of events, as practised in necromancy. In African ancestor veneration, the dead are believed to continue to live and are still regarded as part of the family of the living. They are believed to be the guardians of the living, as well as the mediators between God and the living community. Ancestral veneration is a family affair. This notion is supported by E. Bọlaji Idowu (1973: 186), who suggests that ancestral veneration is essentially a means of communication and communion between the living members of the family and the living-dead. Jean-Marc Elá (1995: 33) points out that offerings made to ancestors are essentially a display of respect and a symbol of the perpetuation of the family line and should therefore be considered an expression of the command to children to love and respect their parents.

The function of the ancestors as active family members and mediators

Choon Sup Bae believes that the relationship between the living-dead and family members is constituted through communication (2007: 32). The living-dead speak with the living through dreams, visions, nature and people. At times they appear to their family members in dreams and at other times only their presence is felt. Often the communication is facilitated by a mediator (diviner, priest, shaman) and in many traditions this position is a very powerful one, enabling the living to consult with the living-dead. Bae sums it up thus:

> The role of the ancestors is closely linked to that of their identity. As being a living part of the community, and often its head or elder, they play a role as the representatives of the social law and tradition, and are construed to be indispensable to uphold the harmony and order within their societies. As seen in their identity, being linked to the Supreme Being, ancestors also play a role as intermediaries or mediators between God and their descendants (2007: 26).

Ancestral veneration, superstitions and social function

Agbonkhianmeghe E. Orobator offers the following description:

> An ancestor is a blood relative of a living community; this relationship could be of common parentage or shared ancestry. The rituals that are performed by family are important to appease the ancestors and must be performed by the member of

the family concerned. These rituals are performed in the sacred places within the home and not just anywhere (2008: 107).

Charles Nyamiti argues that if the ancestors are forgotten or neglected by their descendants, they are said to 'manifest their anger by sending to their descendants bodily or spiritual calamities' (1984: 67). In the African perspective, therefore, illness is an area where the physical and the spiritual meet. There is a fixed relationship between body and soul. Illnesses are usually treated with herbs and concoctions prepared by the *izinyanga* (herbalists) and *izangoma* (diviners), and are often perceived to have been caused by either angry living-dead or an act of witchcraft. The diviners then tell the family members about the cause of the illness and what they should to do to fix the situation.

Accidents are regarded as a reflection of the ancestors' anger towards their living family members, as a result of neglect or unacceptable behaviour within the homestead. The difference between sicknesses induced by the living-dead and witchcraft is that the former puts pressure on the living kin only to frighten them, whereas sorcery is done with an intention to kill them. Sorcery is believed to have been caused by the living-dead when they fail to prevent sickness or misfortune befalling the family because they have been neglected or are angry at an offence. However, it is also believed that sorcery can be caused by witches and sorcerers. S.A. Thorpe contends: 'Pain in the African context is physical with a strong social dimension, not predominantly physical and individualistic. Pain is felt when relationships are disturbed' (1991: 111).

Africans are always interested in knowing the cause of illness. The technique of healing cannot be separated from the symbolic area from which it emerges. Africans emphasise a holistic approach to healing. Ela (1995) and Thorpe (1991) point out that when diagnosing, the healer extends the borders of the disrupted area to include the invisible, mystical level, which leads to a restoration of wholeness on a visible, physical level as well.

I conducted an independent interview with a practising *isangoma* to obtain insight into the living-dead and the role they play in the lives of their living relatives.

Interview with MaZondi, *isangoma* from eMkhambathini, Pietermaritzburg

1. *Amadlozi azilawula kanjani izimpilo zenu emndenini?* (**How do the living-dead control your family lives?**)

    Isibonelo, akwenzisa lokho akufunayo – ayakwazi ukwenza impilo yakho ingaqhubeki ngokushesha, kube nezinkinga.

    Abantu abadala bayahlala kuwe ube namandiki namandawo. Aziveza ngokugula okungachazeki; izibhobo, ukudideka, nokuvele uwe. Kudingeka uthole umuntu owelaphayo akwenzele amagobongo. Uma udla amagobongo awuvunyelwe ukuya ocansini, ukuya ngezicathulo emsamo.

    For example, they make you do what they want you to do. They can cause your life not to prosper as fast as you would want it to; they cause problems. Ancestral spirits possess you. They reveal themselves through unexplainable illnesses, stitches, confusion and fits. You then must find a healer to perform a ritual for you. When you take medication, you are not allowed to engage in sexual intercourse or to wear shoes to the ancestral area at the back of the house.

2. *Yikuphi okwenza uqiniseke ukuthi amadlozi akhulume into ethile?* (**What makes you sure that the living-dead spoke something?**)

    Ubona ngokuthi ube nokugula okungelapheki ngezinto zokwelapha zesiZulu kuchaza ukuthi kumele uyofuna uzwe ukuthi amadlozi athini.

    You realise that when there is an illness that is not curable through traditional medicine, it means that the family needs to consult an *inyanga* or *isangoma* to find out what the ancestors are trying to communicate.

3. *Uma kunokulwa emndenini kugcina sekwenzekeni ngokwamadlozi?* (**When there is fighting in the family, what happens?**)

    Amadlozi awawufuni umsindo. Ningagcina senihlukene, izinto zingahambi kahle. Uma uya kwabelaphayo bakutshele ukuthi konakelephi. Kumele nithelelane amanzi kube nezinto enizenzayo. Kudingeka nilethe izilwane emsamo nixolise kwabalele.

    The living-dead do not appreciate fighting. The family may end up separating, leading to things not going well. When you consult *izinyanga* and *izangoma* they will tell you what is going on. You then must forgive each other and bring animals for sacrifice to apologise to the living-dead.

4. *Kuyenzeka yini ukuthi amadlozi angalwemukeli uxolo?* (**Does it ever happen that the living-dead do not accept the sacrifice?**)

    Kuyenzeka. Uma kuzoba khona ongakwenzi okumisiwe ngokomsamo. Uma kudingeka kukhishwe izilwane yibona bobabili abaxabene ngosuku olulodwa, bese kuba khona onqabayo nongenzi okubekiwe.

    It happens. When the family members do not do as instructed. When there is a need for both parties to offer animals on the same day, then one of them refuses to do as instructed.

5. *Kuyenzeka yini amadlozi akhiphe isidumbu?* (Do the living-dead sometimes kill people?)
   Yebo, uma umsindo uwacasule kakhulu amadlozi. Uma bekunesimo obekumele nisigweme noma uma ningaxoli ngokuphelele. Idlozi alishayi umuntu owonile kodwa lishaya oseceleni.
   Yes, when fighting angers them. When there is something that could have been avoided or when you do not forgive each other sincerely. The living-dead do not punish the culprit but the innocent person.

6. *Imuphi umehluko oba khona ezehlakalweni ezejwayelekile nje nezenziwa amadlozi?* (What is the difference between normal accidents and those caused by the living-dead)?
   Kuyavela uma umuntu elimala, amadlozi ayasho ukuthi lokhu kudalwe yini. Uma umuntu ebetshelwe into bese engayenzi noma labo abathembisa izinto isib. Ukuthi uzohlabela ingane imbuzi yomhlonyane, idlozi liyadinwa uma ungasakwenzi.
   It becomes clear when a person gets injured, the living-dead will always shed light as to the cause of the accident. When a person was told to do something and did not or those who promise to sacrifice for the ancestors and do not, as in the name, when a parent promised to slaughter a goat to announce the coming-of-age ceremony, the living-dead get angry when you do not do it.

7. *Izinto ezicasula amadlozi.* (Things that anger the living-dead).
   Umsindo, ukulinunusela ngokudla bese ungahlabi, lapho lihleli khona alibafuni abantu abajabulisana ngokocansi. Imisindo yabantu abakhulumela phezulu noma umsakazo. Elinye alizifuni izicathulo, lifuna ushuqule, umboze amahlombe.
   Fighting, saying you will make a sacrifice and then not do it, and where the living-dead live they do not want people who engage in sex. People speaking in loud voices and turning on the radio is strictly forbidden in the ancestral area. They do not like shoes, and if you are a woman you must cover your head and shoulders.

8. *Uma ungaliniki ukudla liyakubulala yini?* (If you do not sacrifice for the living-dead, can they kill you?)
   Uma izizukulwane bezihlaba wena usukhetha ukungahlabi kuba nezinto ezimbi ezenzekayo.
   If your predecessors used to sacrifice and you choose to change that, bad things might happen.

9. *Ukulwa kwabafazi bendoda eyodwa kwenzani edlozini?* (What does the fighting between co-wives do to the living-dead?)
   Liyadinwa idlozi. Kumele indoda ibe nezinto ezenzayo, ibethule emsamo, ibahlanganise. Uma bethukana egcekeni kufanele bahlawule ngoba bahlambaza idlozi. Kumele bageze umuzi, ngoba uma bengahlawuli kungavela umkhuhlane kubona noma ezinganeni zabo.

> The living-dead get angry. The husband must perform some rituals and introduce them to the living-dead, and use *umuthi* (medicine) to make them get along with each other. If they shout at each other within the homestead they must apologise because they are embarrassing the living-dead. The co-wives must cleanse the homestead, because if they do not apologise there might be some misfortune, their children might get sick.

This is a clear indication that ancestors play a pivotal role in guardianship over family members. They reward good behaviour and punish 'wrongdoers'. Despite the complex nature of the relationships within polygynous families, individuals are expected to avoid fighting and confronting one another, as this behaviour angers the ancestors. When the family members die, they do not disappear, but live on in both the spiritual and the physical realm. They communicate directly with God on behalf of their family members and at the same time they are part of their living family members.

Socialisation is an important part of venerating and appeasing the living-dead. What the society prescribes is what individuals grow up to adopt and conform to. Ancestral rituals are events that take place within a particular society and individuals within that community observe these without question. Noleen Turner argues:

> Whatever the values and norms of a society are, they are passed on to its members from generation to generation as they mature. This maturation process, which takes place in all societal groups, is a matter of learning how to adjust one's behaviour and expectations in relation to other members of one's group. To a certain degree, this involves observing the patterns of behaviour of those around you, what is done and not done, what evokes pleasure or displeasure. In part, it involves expressly being taught what is 'right' and what is 'wrong' in terms of values for that particular community (2003: 89).

Burial rites

In most African societies there is a great emphasis placed on how a person is buried. It is believed that, for instance, if a person disappears and dies without his family's knowledge and does not get a proper burial, his soul lingers on the earth and he is always seen at night, troubling passers-by. Burial is the most common method of dealing with a corpse. John Mbiti states: 'Some societies bury the body inside the house where the person was living at the time of death; others bury it in the compound where the homestead is situated; others bury the body behind the compound; and some do it at the place where the person was born' (1969: 154). He further notes that 'people view death paradoxically: it is a separation but not annihilation, the dead person is suddenly cut off from the human society and yet the corporate group clings to him'. Certain rituals must be performed for a person to be at peace and to cross over. Simon Bockie observes the importance of performing rituals:

> Spiritually, the dead remain part of the old living community as well as the new community of the living-dead, until all the rites of adjustment to his departure are properly observed and completed. In the meantime, he remains a public charge to those closely related to him, a public charge in the sense that they adjust their way of life according to his present status namely, 'betweenness'. While on the one hand he belongs to both communities, the living and the dead, on the other hand, he belongs to neither. He is a member without identity (1993: 106).

The destiny of the soul

African people believe strongly that their dead family members are not gone and that the spirits of their dead look after them. They can feel their presence. Birago Diop, a Senegalese poet, observes in his poem 'Sighs' that in Africa:

> . . . Those who are dead are never gone:
>   They are there in the thickening shadow.
> The dead are not under the earth:
>   They are in the tree that rustles,
>   They are in the wood that groans;
> Those who are dead are never gone:
>   They are in the breast of the woman,

>   They are in the child who is wailing
>   And in the firebrand that flames.
> The dead are not under the earth:
>   They are in the forest,
>   They are in the house
> The dead are not dead (cited in Olupona 2000: 54).

The implication of this poem is that the living-dead do not leave their families. They always linger on to look after and guard their living relatives. Their bodies are buried underground, but that is not the destiny of their souls. They are everywhere ('They are in the breast of the woman / They are in the child who is wailing'). There is a belief that when a family member dies their soul is reincarnated in newborn babies. 'They are in the house' links to the *ukubuyisa* ritual that brings the dead back home after a year of mourning.

The living-dead are aware of everything that is happening with their living relatives and they intervene when necessary, at their own discretion. Frederick I. Danquah says of the Akan living-dead: 'They act as friends at court to intervene between man and the Supreme Being, and to get prayers and petitions answered more quickly and effectively' (cited in Olupona 2000: 55). The living-dead may give instructions, or enquire about the family, or make requests to be given something, and may even threaten to punish family members for not carrying out particular instructions or for not caring sufficiently for the living-dead.

African people are generally eager to please their living-dead and to keep a good relationship with them. This relationship continues for as long as someone who knew them is alive. According to Mbiti (1969), people who think that the hereafter is in another world or a distant place bury food and weapons with the dead body to sustain and protect the person on the journey between the two worlds. For many people, however, the next world is geographically 'here', being separated from this earth only by virtue of being invisible to human beings. As soon as the funeral rites are performed, the soul begins its journey. There are many African people who do not visualise any geographical separation between the two worlds. As soon as a person is physically dead, he arrives 'there' in a spirit form. This means that a person is thought to be composed of physical and spiritual entities, and among some societies to these is added 'a shadow' and 'a breath' or 'a personality'.

Mbiti (1969) further states that there is no concrete evidence of the hereafter being pictured in terms of punishment or reward. For many African people, the hereafter is only a continuation of life as it was in its human form. This means that personalities are retained, social and political status maintained, sex distinction is continued, human activities are reproduced in the hereafter, the wealth or poverty of the individual remains unchanged and, in many ways, the hereafter is a carbon copy of the present life. African people both acknowledge and deny the disruption of death. A person dies and yet he continues to live. The surviving relatives hold on to the deceased and they remember him.

Powers of the living-dead

The living-dead also mediate between this world and the spirit world. They play a large part in most African cultures, are easily accessible and are generally considered benevolent. When alive, these living-dead led lives judged to be honourable and well respected. They are well placed to give advice and warnings. They are, in many ways, as real to the people who talk to them, as the living. Placide Tempels (1959) believes that the African world view is centred on what he calls a 'vital force'. For him, Africans conceptualise 'being' as that which has force, and force is the nature of being. From this he derives that African behaviour is geared towards achieving, or improving, the life force in their favour. Similarly, Edwin W. Smith states:

> *Muntu*, 'person', signifies the vital force endowed with intelligence and will; *bintu*, are what we call things in Bantu philosophy, forces not endowed with reason. Above all forces is God, who gives existence and increase to all others. After him come the first fathers, who are the founders of all clans, from the chain binding God and man. These occupy a rank so high that they are no longer considered human. Next to them come the 'living-dead' of the tribe who are links in the chain, through which the vital force influences the living generation. The living, in turn, form their hierarchy according to their vital power. The eldest of

a clan is the link between the living-dead and their descendants (1950: 18).

According to Christopher Vecsey, the Baluba of the Congo in Central Africa believe in the existence of a 'power' from which life emanates (cited in Akijar 2000). The Baluba conceive of this power as the source of vital force. All visible and invisible beings, as well as death, are caused by this power. Vecsey's findings show that life among the Baluba is supported by this vital force, which grows as a person ages in life, through to its climax at their death. However, it can either diminish or increase depending upon the way in which one conducts oneself. Vecsey further writes:

> The deceased's vital force persists into the afterlife, but after death it can no longer increase itself as it can while the person is alive. It – the vital force, the dead person or the ancestor – relies on the living to maintain its strength, and its eventual fate is almost certain diminishment over time. The dead person, then, consists of a vital force which has reached its peak of strength. It can influence the living, but it has now become independent upon its name, since the living will maintain their ancestor's strength through offerings only as long as they remember the deceased's named identity (cited in Akijar 2000: 30).

It is a collective responsibility of every member of the family to maintain and strengthen the vital force. The life of an individual in African societies is a shared societal life. Individuals within the community are aware that they do not live for themselves. For Africans, life without living within and with the community is meaningless.

The living-dead
Zulu people have different names through which they address their living-dead, as indicated in the table below.

Amadlozi	Living-dead
Abaphansi	The ones beneath
Izidalwa	Mysterious creatures – they do not have their bodies, yet they are alive

Izithutha	The not so clever ones – because if something angers them, there is usually very little one can do about their reaction
Abalele	The ones who have gone to sleep
Abangasekho	The ones who have departed
Amathongo	Ancestral spirits
Asebethule	The ones who have gone quiet
Amakhosi	Kings (term used by *izangoma*)

The living-dead are the core of African religions. They are African people's guardian angels. They act as go-betweens for the Supreme Being and their living family members. African people are always at the mercy of their living-dead. When something good happens to them, such as finding a job, they thank their living-dead accordingly. When something bad happens, it is seen as a punishment from the living-dead, something they need to apologise for.

African people cannot neglect their living-dead, as this may have serious repercussions for them and their families. The living-dead are regarded as spirits in the sense that they are no longer visible (Uka 1991: 29). Nana Afia Opoku-Asare says that ancestral belief acts as a form of social control, through which the conduct of individuals is regulated (cited in Olupona 2000: 55). The constant reminder of the good deeds of the living-dead acts as a spur for good conduct on the part of the living, and the belief that the dead can punish those who violate traditionally sanctioned mores acts as a deterrent. Ancestral beliefs, therefore, represent a powerful source of moral sanction and affirm the values upon which the society is based.

An incident that reflects the danger of angering the living-dead can be seen in I.S. Kubheka's book *Ulaka lwabaNguni* (The Wrath of the Nguni People). Here, a young man named Mphakamiseni (lift him up) had forsaken his parents because they were illiterate. He changed his name to McPherson. He was a well-known doctor who went to university through his mother's hard work, but he could not associate himself with low-life people (his parents). When he got married, he wanted children, but could not have them. He was supposed to go home and ask for forgiveness from his mother (*ukushweleza*). Kubheka says:

> *UMphakamiseni wazizwa efikelwa yisibindi wezwa ukuthi uzonqoba futhi. Wayesengene kwesinye isikole manje, isikole okungesona esencwadi. Yinye kuphela impi okwakufanele ayinqobe manje, yimpi yolaka lwabaNguni, okwakuyimpi yolaka lukanina uBazothini . . . umbhemu lona uma efuna ukushweleza ngesiZulu kumele makaphindele ezimpandeni zakhe angazami ukukha phezulu, kwakufanele aye ekhaya eMnambithi. Futhi ngoba wayeseke wakhuluma ngalolu daba kwakungasafanele achithe isikhathi, hleze izithutha zithukuthelele.*

Mphakamiseni was courageous and saw his victory. It was a war he had to conquer. He entered a new school which was not about reading books. He had one last war to conquer, the war of the wrath of the Nguni people, which was the war of his mother's wrath . . . If the young man wanted to apologise in the Zulu way, he would have to go to his roots. He was supposed to go home to Mnambithi [Ladysmith]. Because he had already spoken about it, he then had a duty to do it, otherwise the living-dead would become angry at him (1988: 214).

It is clear from the above incident that the living-dead demand unquestioning respect from their living family members. Werner Eiselen and Isaac Schapera summarise this best when they say:

> The good and moral man in Bantu society is the one who honours the ancestors by living as they have lived. Nevertheless, most of what we consider to be evil is forbidden also in Bantu society, and what we hold to be good is also recommended by them. The Bantu would, in fact, have no difficulty in accepting most of the Biblical commandments, because among them, too, the danger of taking the name of a god in vain is generally acknowledged; reverence for parents and those in authority is commonly inculcated, men of probity are respected; brotherliness, courtesy, and hospitality are common virtues; A high respect for property prevails; mercy is highly esteemed and justice praised; murder, witchcraft, stealing, adultery, bearing false witness against one's neighbour, hatred and arrogance are all condemned; and there is such a sense of family responsibility that orphans and destitute

people are provided for. But there is a fundamental difference between their approach, and ours, to the problem of moral goodness: the Bantu demand moral behaviour within the family and tribe rather than moral behaviour in general. And this is in complete harmony with their ancestor worship, for the common ancestor must, of necessity, resent any action by one of his descendants likely to harm another descendant and incidentally to upset the social order within the group (1950: 87).

The sanctity of an African name

To an African, a name is a sacred thing. That is why children are forbidden to call their elders by their names. Alex Kidd says that Zulu people 'will often try to put you off when you enquire about the meaning of a name by saying, "A name is a name and nothing more." Yet it is frequently a great deal more' (cited in Koopman 1986: 15). As S.M.E. Bhengu points out: 'Through the name, an individual is linked up with the ancestors and the spirit world. In this way an African name is a human form of identification that puts one in an uninterrupted continuity with his past and the gods' (1975: 52).

John Henderson Soga has this to say about Xhosa people:

> It is taboo to shout out a man's name when calling him either during the day or the night. The objection is on the score partly that it is derogatory to the dignity of a man to shout out his name . . . Shouting out the name of an individual enables the sorcerer (*umthakathi*) to become familiar with it, and some night when he desires to work evil on the person named he will shout out the name, with the consequence that he who has been called will wake up in the morning with constricted vocal cords and be unable to articulate clearly (cited in Koopman 1986: 16).

The connection between a person's name and the dangers of witchcraft or sorcery are discussed more fully in Chapter 6.

4

Names and Social Identity in the Zulu Naming System

Ihechukwu Madubuike asserts:

> Some people say there is nothing in a name. This is a grossly misleading statement. It is difficult to think of anything one can do today without making use of a name. In our modern society, with its strong economic structure, a man who has no name is a man who has nothing. People, organisational groups, businesses of various kinds, are all identified by one kind of name or another. Countries, towns, cities and villages are all identified by names (1976: 7).

Names are used to project individual identity and also reveal the affiliations that family members have in their social lives. Identity gives name-bearers a location in the community and links them with the society they live in. As Charles Pfukwa and Lawrie Barnes point out:

> A name is a social peg; it expresses a cultural or social perspective of the name or the owner of the name. Naming and renaming becomes an act of claiming and rewriting an identity. To name the self is a declaration of independence from wider social control and it is a choice in identity (2008: 98–9).

Concerning the link between names and identity, Ogonna Chuks-Orji says: 'Indeed, it is not until a child has been named that he [or she] is considered a person' (1972: 82). Social identity theorists argue that because people define themselves in terms of their social group membership and enact roles as part of their acceptance of the normative expectations of in-group members, the concept of individual role is subsumed under the concept of group (Turner 1994). John E. Joseph explains: 'Group identities, particularly national and ethnic identities . . . fulfill the positive function of giving people a sense of who they are, of belonging to a community, in the absence of which one can feel a sense of alienation that can bring disastrous consequences' (2004: 46). Being part of a group is a salient phenomenon in Zulu culture, which causes individuals to feel accepted and raises their self-esteem. This entails a specific role that individuals must play within the group. Sheldon Stryker (1980) emphasises that identity theory affects self-esteem as well as self-efficacy. If an individual performs their role positively, their self-esteem grows (Hoelter 1985). If the individual plays their role well, the individual feels accepted by the group (Franks and Marolla 1976).

Individual identity versus social identity

Speaking about surnames in a Western context, W.F.H. Nicolaisen remarks:

> Whether our name is patronymic like Jones, for instance, or an occupational name like Smith, or a descriptive nickname like Brown, or of local origin like Washington, it is unlikely to identify us as the son of John, a shoer of horses, a person with brown hair, or someone from Washington, England. In our society we have lived with inherited surnames for so long that we regard them at best as genealogical markers, or more probably as mere onomastic labels, even when to the etymologically uninitiated they are semantically quite transparent and betray their origin without much probing (1976: 144).

In contrast, in an African context, as far back as 1931, John Henderson Soga (1860–1941), son of the famous Tiyo Soga, and a minister, translator, historian and ethnographer, emphasised:

> There are two forces which bind all tribes of the Bantu into a racial unit. The first is spiritual as exemplified in the religion, and in the spirit world wherein dwell the spirits of the ancestral chiefs,

and of each family's departed relatives . . . The second force is relationship, which works through the kinship of a progenitor, and through a common blood stream reaching to the furthest off descendants; thus, binding the progenitor to the family, clan and tribe which have being in him, and likewise binding family, clan and tribe to him (1931: 7–8).

From an African perspective, identity involves communal living and the concept of ubuntu, a unifying vision inspired by the Zulu proverb '*Umuntu ngumuntu ngabantu*' (a person is a person through other people). Although this proverb has become seen by some as a cliché, the concept of ubuntu has been revived and has thus received significant attention since the call made by the former president of South Africa, Thabo Mbeki, for an African Renaissance and his 'I am an African' speech made in 1996. African people are communal and before one can examine an individual identity it should be remembered that an individual functions within a community. Criticism does not deter staunch believers in the concept from practising ubuntu. In Zulu society, people live a communal life, in which everybody belongs and is part of a group. In acknowledging the communal dimension of the African way of life, John Mbiti states:

> In traditional life, the individual does not and cannot exist alone except corporately. He owes this existence to other people, including those of past generations and his contemporaries. He is simply part of the whole. The community must therefore make, create or produce the individual; for the individual depends on the corporate group . . . whatever happens to the individual happens to the whole group happens to the individual. The individual can only say 'I am, because we are; and since we are, therefore I am'. This is the cardinal point in the understanding of the African view of man (1969: 108).

It is still true that in Zulu social discourse, social and personal identities are intertwined. They feature socio-cognitive processes of self-categorisation and depersonalisation. Identity theory focuses on the behaviour of everyone within a group. It focuses on the causes and consequences of identifying with a particular role. Being a member of a group primarily means that there are implications regarding one's actions. For example, social identity theory emphasises one's identification and association with a particular racial group, while identity theory examines the roles or behaviours people enact as members of a racial group (Mutran and Burke 1979; White and Burke 1987).

Names single out people and identify name-bearers. They indicate the uniqueness of a particular individual and mark an individual in a group. The meaning of a name assigns a bundle of characteristics to a name; it provides background, behaviour and the abilities of the name-bearer. The identity of each person is unique, but names are only unique in a context where there are no other people with the same name. A name gives the name-bearer a sense of identity within the society.

This chapter examines the primary meaning (referential and denotative) and the secondary meaning (emotive and connotative) of names. Names in their primary function refer to, denote and identify the name-bearer. The secondary function is communicative and externalisation of conflict, which is more relevant to this book. This chapter also explores how choosing a particular name acts as a link to polygyny, family structure and the state of mind of the parents at the time of the birth.

Euro-Western and African names

Nicolaisen maintains that few parents in Europe or in European-derived societies name their children because they are aware of the lexical meaning of a name and deem it appropriate, and that 'despite many books of the *How to Name Your Baby* variety, it is doubtful whether there are many Margaret's, Bridget's, and William's around who were so named because they were thought to be "pearls", "high goddesses", or "helmets of resolution"' (1976: 154). Robert K. Herbert and Senni Bogatsu (2001: 3) comment: 'The criterion most often employed in distinguishing African and Western names is that of name meaningfulness. It is well known that African names "have meaning" and speakers readily identify that meaning. Western names, on the other hand, are very largely devoid of meaning for modern speakers.' In their research, Joyce Mathangwane and Sheena Gardner found that many people had a strong negative attitude towards English names because they are perceived not to have any meaning. They maintain:

> While many of the respondents with English names simply responded that they did not know the meaning of their names, it was interesting to find that some have invented their own meanings based on the phonological features of the name e.g. someone called Analysa gives the meaning as 'someone who analyses' (Mathangwane and Gardner 1998: 81–2).

As an example, I prefer to use my African name, Bonisiwe – the one who has been given a vision – rather than my first name, Evangeline. For many years I did not even know what this name meant. My Grade 6 teacher shortened it to Vangeli (the gospel) and children would call me Evangelini (in the gospel) and I would hate it. It was not until I was doing Latin studies at university that the lecturer asked me if I knew what my name meant. When I said no, he told me that it meant 'the deliverer of good news'. I was delighted to finally know the meaning of my name, but still prefer my African name, by which I am well known. For me, the African name sounds better than a Greek-origin Latin name that has very little to do with who I am. As Heinrich Albert Wieschhoff, discussing African names, says: 'Names are not merely considered as tags by means of which individuals may be distinguished, but are intimately associated with various events in the life of the individual as well as those of the family and the larger social groups' (1941: 212).

The meaning of African names

African names have a literal meaning and there is usually a story behind the name: why the name was given and what circumstances surrounded the birth of that child. Samuel Gyasi Obeng contends:

> African names are important channels for speaking for and about African societies. They are used to achieve a number of goals, including showing human relationships and social roles, revealing Africans' quests for truth and meaning in life, showing

the polarity – e.g. goodness and badness – in human behaviour, pointing to the name users' (name-givers and name-bearers) hopes, dreams and aspirations, showing African perceptions of cosmic elements like the sun, moon, wind and rain, and many others. African names may reflect the name-user's geographical environment, as well as their fears, religious beliefs and philosophies of life and death. Children's names may even provide insights into important cultural or socio-political events at the time of their birth (2001: 1).

Speaking about African names, Madubuike notes:

Names given to people have definite meanings, and parents, relatives, and well-wishers are very conscious when choosing the names of their children or of an individual. Thus, names are not merely labels that individuals carry along with them. They have a deep social significance and many names studied collectively express a world view (1976: 13–14).

Julia Stewart emphasises the importance of giving a child an ethnic name:

Giving a child or yourself an ethnic name can be an important step in reaffirming cultural pride. Names are not just words, they are a link to all the ancestors who came before you and all the progeny who will follow. Traditional African names have a wonderful meaning and unique histories. With a mere mention of an African name, one can conjure up images of vast savannahs and endless deserts, dense forests and palm-fringed beaches, of golden ancient kingdoms and proud warriors, of spirited music and dance, of urban hustle-bustle and rural tranquility. Most of all one can imagine the smiling faces of children who will carry their revived ethnic traditions to the next generation (1993: viii).

Chuks-Orji claims: 'Yoruba people of Nigeria have a saying: "we consider our state of affairs before we name a child". This attitude is general throughout Africa, and so, since Africans are extremely fond of children, a birth in the family is, as a rule, an occasion for rejoicing' (1972: 75).

Choosing a name

African people choose names that are relevant to their status, state of mind, situation and circumstances at the time of birth. People must view the world through the eyes of the name-giver, consider things from their perspective and perceive the injustices reflected in that name as strongly as the name-giver does. Obeng notes: 'Name bearers thus act as a means through which the messages inherent in their names are transmitted from sources to their targets. A name-bearer thus acts as a pseudo-epicentre or a pseudo-addressee' (2001: 5). He adds:

> There is a great deal of intertextualization, that is, borrowing from previous anthroponyms, as well as utilizing public knowledge, in creating names. There are also intertextual relations existing between different names and between some names and the public knowledge accessible to members within and without the speech communities. In choosing a name, the name-givers take their life histories, occupational and social domains, public knowledge, geographical location, and the cultural conventions on communication into consideration. The names are thus a reaction to, and a reflection of, all or some of the above facts. Also, because contexts within which African names are created play an important role in their interpretation, detaching names from their contexts could distort their pragmatic import or even subject them to multiple interpretation and misinterpretation (Obeng 2001: 5).

African names are thus anchored in sociocultural discourse and are connected to the everyday life of the name-givers. They situate meaning in local sociocultural and communicative contexts, so, in order to understand them or give appropriate context-sensitive interpretations to them, one needs to take into consideration the name-giver's world view, as well as the world view of the other discourse participants and the wider community. In African society, the naming of a child is a matter of great importance. Several considerations influence the choice of the name or names to be given. Chuks-Orji reveals:

> The naming of a child, then, has as its purpose the recognition of a new personal presence incarnate within the community. The ceremonies and customs associated with birth lead the child normally and naturally to his absorption into the community in which he will ultimately, as an adult, find his personal fulfillment through his active functioning in the total society (1972: 77).

Chuks-Orji emphasises that 'in the African tradition, today as yesterday, a name is not a mere identification tag. It is a record of family and community history, a distinct personal reference, an indication of present status and an enunciated promise of future accomplishment' (1972: 86).

The name-giver

In Zulu society, as in most African societies, names are in most cases chosen by the mothers. In many instances, the mother is the one who stays at home with the child, bringing up the children. In polygynous families, mothers are usually the ones with issues to voice, so it has become accepted that mothers are in most cases the name-givers. H.O. Mönnig says of the Pedi:

> The child now receives its first babyhood name. The name is usually chosen by the mother, but will finally have to be decided on by the family of the father, and particularly by his eldest sister. This is indicative of her position of influence over her brother's children, and, if it is a daughter, of her having a claim on this girl as a future bride for her son (1967: 103).

However, it is not always African women who are the name-givers. John Beattie describes the custom of the Nyoro people thus: 'The personal name may be given by either parent or even by a grandparent or other relative, but if the father is known and present he generally has the last word' (cited in Koopman 1986: 32).

Names in isiZulu are thought out and carefully planned. During a woman's pregnancy, family members have enough time to view their situations and then choose a suitable name for the child. Names commemorating the living-dead are used in some families, as in the name Nhlanhla (luck), because that name belonged to the child's grandfather. The following are some of the categories of names that are usually found in KwaMambulu:

Historical events	Nomkhumbi (mother of ships)
Political events	Ntandoyeningi (democracy)
God-related names	Thembelenkosini (trusting in God) Velemseni (a gift from the grace)
	Cebolenkosi (God's plan)
Educated parents	Nomfundo (mother of education)
	Nokwazi (mother of knowledge)
	Lwazi (knowledge)
Gratefulness	Nokubonga (mother of gratefulness) Sibongiseni (be thankful with us)
Order of the children	Ntombintathu (three girls) Zimbili (two girls) Ntombifuthi (another girl) Mfanafuthi (another boy)
Happiness	Ntokozo (joy) Nonjabulo (mother of joy)
Appearance	Buhlebethu (our beauty) Sibahlesonke (we are all beautiful)
Trust	Thembekile (the faithful one) Sethembene (we trust each other) Nokwethemba (the mother of trust)
Love	Noluthando (mother of love) Thandanani (love each other)

Progress	Thuthukani (develop yourselves) Nqubeko (progress)
Comfort	Nduduzo (comfort) Duduzile (she has given us comfort) Mduduzi (comforter)
Pride	Baqhenyile (they are proud)
Ilobolo	Zibuyile (they have returned)
Clan names	Zamahlomuka (the girls of the Hlomuka clan) Hlabangane (Mtshali clan praise name) Bhekamabomvu (the Ngubane clan praise name)
Disappointment	Zehlile (their cheeks have dropped) Bajabhile (they were disappointed)
Enough children	Anele (they are enough) Kwanele (it is enough) Sanele (we are enough)
Appreciating the gift	Simphiwe (he has been given to us) Baphiwe (they have been given) Aphiwe (they have been given)
Days	Nomgqibelo (mother of Saturdays) Nomasonto (mother of Sundays)

The meaning of names

It has been argued that a proper name is an unmeaning mark, which we connect in our minds with the idea of the object, in order that whenever the mark meets our eyes or occurs in our thoughts, we may think of that individual object (Mill, cited in Gardiner 1957: 38). The reason that some linguists conclude that proper names do not have meaning is because in some names, the meaning is not easily recognisable. Peter E. Raper asserts:

> There may be several reasons why the 'meanings' of names are not always readily discernible. The name, or part of the name, may be in an unknown language; the name may be so old that the word(s) from which it is derived are no longer in current use; the name may have been so greatly adapted (some say 'corrupted') that it is no longer recognizable (1987: 17).

On the other hand, Noleen Turner argues: 'Among the Zulu people, not only do names serve as useful labels to distinguish one particular person from another in the community or society at large, they also reflect the occurrence of certain natural or historic events commensurate with the birth of the child' (1992: 43).

Holger Steen Sørensen has identified the meaning of a proper name as the designatum, the sound sequence as the designator and the entity referred to as the denotatum. He contends:

> The extra linguistic entity or entities we refer to by means of a sign 'S', I call the denotatum or denotata of S. The denotata of 'a mother' are well-known entities of flesh and blood which have given birth to at least one child. 'A mother' denotes (applies to, is used of) these entities. The denotatum of 'Churchill', the extra linguistic entity Churchill, the person Churchill (cited in Raper 1987: 78).

Commenting on Sørensen's theory, Mbali Machaba has this to say:

> Sørensen's theory also poses challenges where one has to analyse the designator. It is conceivable that some names, especially of geographical entities, are old as human history can be traced, and as a result the designator is not easily discernible. This is challenging when one has to analyse those names as linguistic signs. It should be taken into account that some names are adopted from languages different to that of the community where the name is found. These names in most cases go through some phonological adaptations when they are adopted by the receiving language (2005: 31).

Lexical meaning

'Lexical meaning' is the basic meaning of the speech parts that constitute the name; it is sometimes also called 'literal meaning' (Louwrens 1993). The lexical meaning of a name is concerned with the original meaning, before the word becomes a name: it is still regarded as a pure linguistic item that can be subjected to the rigours of linguistic analysis (Louwrens 1993). Below are some examples:

Zulu name	Lexical meaning
Hlengiwe	the redeemed
Zizile	they (girls) have come
Nozipho	mother of gifts
Smangele	we are surprised
Nontobeko	mother of respect
Lindiwe	the awaited one
Skhumbuzo	reminder
Slondiwe	we have been saved
Sinqobile	we have conquered
Khumbula	remember

In their language of origin, names have lexical meaning, but when they move into other languages they become lexically opaque (Neethling 1995). Names like Ruby (a precious stone), Pearl (valuable jewel) or Regina (a queen) given to isiZulu-speaking women have become lexically opaque (to isiZulu speakers), which causes some people to think they are meaningless. However, apart from lexical meaning, names also have a referential and inferential meaning.

Referential and inferential meaning

Reference deals with the relationship between the linguistic elements, words, sentences and the non-linguistic world of experience (Palmer 1981: 29). Raper (1983: 68) notes that reference is the most important function of a name. Successful reference depends on hearers identifying the speaker's intended referent, based on the referring expression used (Brown and Yule 1983: 205). Let us look at the following short imaginary dialogue to illustrate this point:

> Four boys are seated on a bench under a tree. One of their mothers calls her son:

Mama: Mkhipheni!
Mkhipheni: Mama?
Mama: *Woz'othatha nali elinye ibhentshi* (Come and take another bench).
Mkhipheni: (*Ethatha ibhentshi*) (Takes the bench). *Siyabonga Mama* (Thank you Mom).

This short dialogue shows that the name Mkhipheni identifies the referent (the boy by the name of Mkhipheni) out of the four boys. When his mother calls out the name there is no confusion as to who she is referring to. John R. Searle (1969: 87) proposes that a necessary condition of a speaker's intention to refer to a particular object or a person in the utterance of an expression is the speaker's ability to provide an 'identifying description' of that object. For the hearer to identify whatever the speaker is referring to, the speaker's utterance must either be, or be supplemented by, an identifying description. With regard to the use of proper names in particular, Searle (1969: 171) contends that when a name is uttered, both the speaker and hearer associate some identifying description with it; that is, a certain aspect of the name's descriptive backing, so that the particular reference that was intended by the use of the name is successfully achieved.

The knowledge of sociocultural issues helps inference. For instance, let us consider the boy's name Bonabeganwa (he sees others getting married). This boy's uncle (*ubab' omncane*) saw his brother marrying many wives and thought that he could also manage a polygynous family, while in fact he had no idea about what being a polygynist would entail. The father of the boy gave his son this name to mock his younger brother for trying to do something he could not afford. In Zulu culture, not every man is encouraged to be polygynous. It is for a man who has enough cattle to pay *ilobolo* for each wife and enough wealth to support all his wives and their children.

Pragmatic meaning
According to Raper (1987: 81), pragmatic (or associative) meaning consists of four different types of meaning: connotative, affective or emotive, social or stylistic and phonic associative. Connotative meaning

includes things known about the entity referred to. Affective or emotive meaning results from individual emotions (good or bad) a person may feel towards an entity.

Connotative meaning addresses the four elements of a naming system: a name, a name-bearer, a name-giver and the context within which the names are used. For example, the name Thangithini (what do you want me to say?) was given to a girl by the father within a polygynous homestead because he did not know how to intervene when his wives were always fighting over petty issues. The following table gives more examples of such names:

Name	Name-bearer	Name-giver	Context
Hlebani (what are you gossiping about?)	A girl	The grandmother	The mother of this girl was always gossiping about people
Magamakhe (in her own words)	A boy	The mother	Her co-wives were denying what they had said about her
Fihlwaphi (where are we going to hide her?)	A girl	The grandmother	There were suspicions of the use of witchcraft by co-wives
Mthethokayizwani (rules are conflicting)	A boy	The father	His elder son was making his own rules within the homestead

Apart from having meaning, names function to identify people and convey messages to intended people and to externalise conflict within the families of name-bearers.

Underlying meanings and perceptions
The underlying meaning of a name informs the way in which people perceive the name and the name-bearer. This leads to stereotypical perceptions of that name and stereotypical expectations of the name-bearer's lifestyle and achievements in life. Richard Gamble (1996)

discusses in detail the notion of stereotyping and describes a process of prejudging a person. He makes it clear that this process is the basis of stereotyped prejudices. In some cases, the name-bearer is perceived negatively because a certain part of the name sounds negative. This can be seen in the following examples: Sonosakhe (his sin) and Khalazome (they will cry until they run out of tears). The noun *isono* (sin), in the first name and the verb *-khala* (cry), in the second name, conjure up negative feelings in people and, as a result, they perceive both names negatively. Coincidentally, in this case, the name-bearers happen to be a housebreaker and a bank robber respectively. The context in which these names were bestowed is not taken into consideration when a perception is formed. The name Sonosakhe was given by the single mother whose husband deserted her when she was pregnant and she felt that it was sinful of him to do that. The name Khalazome was given by the mother because her child was handsome. She was implying that when maidens see him they will cry because they will all wish he was their husband. In both instances, the names are perceived negatively by the community, but the intentions and the expectations of the name-givers are positive.

The underlying meaning of a name can differ from how the community perceives the name. I find parallels between 'wishful' and 'survival' names. Wishful names reflect the parents' choice of a name for their newborn child and the kind of life parents hope their children will lead. The following table provides examples:

Name	Hope
Nobuhle (mother of beauty)	That the name-bearer will be a beautiful person
Nompumelelo (mother of success)	That the name-bearer will be successful in everything she does
Nomfundo (mother of education)	That the name-bearer will be intelligent and well educated

Even though it is believed that a name shapes the life of the name-bearer, this is not the case all the time. It should be noted that parents' wishes are not always realised. There are people with the name Nompumelelo who are not successful and those with the name Nobuhle who are not beautiful. On the other hand, survival names are aimed at confusing evil spirits and witches into thinking that the name-bearer is not wanted. The table below reflects this point:

Name	Perception
Mzondeni (hate him)	That his parents do not love him and that they want everybody to hate him as well
Mzibeni (ignore him)	That his parents do not pay attention to him and they want the community to do the same
Mlahleni (desert him)	That his parents expect everybody to desert him

The underlying meaning of a name informs the way in which the community perceives it. In the case of survival names, negative perceptions do not change the expectations of the parents and the hopes they have for their children to live better lives.

Function of names
Naming and identity
On the primary function of names, Tim Brennen defines identity as 'a relatively stable self-picture, which consists of the opinions, attitudes, habits and beliefs that last relatively unchanged over long periods of time' (2000: 144).

A person's name is a valuable clue to their nationality or mother tongue, which is also part of their identity. This is evident, for example, in the names Lufuno ('love' in Tshivenda); Nombeko ('mother of respect' in isiXhosa) and Puleng ('in the rain' in SeSotho). At societal level, names can tell us much about gender (Nobuhle – mother of beauty); religion (Sihlezinenkosi – we live with the Lord); class (Nomfundo – mother of education – which reflects neutrality and sophistication).

The bestowal of a name is a symbolic contract between the society and the individual. From one side of the contract, by bestowing the name, the society confirms the individual's existence as well as acknowledging its responsibilities towards the name-bearer. The name differentiates the child from others; thus, the society will be able to treat and deal with the child as someone with needs and feelings different from those of other people. Through the name, the individual becomes part of the history of the society and, because of the name, his or her deeds will exist separately from the deeds of others.

On the secondary function of names, Alan Dundes (1983) and John Joseph (2004) claim that identity is a reciprocal process that operates at two levels:
- how the individual or group projects or perceives itself;
- how the reader or recipient perceives the projected identity.

The table below reflects both the projected and perceived identities:

Name	Projected identity: by name-giver and name-bearer	Perceived identity: by the community
Nkabenkulu (the great hitman)	A dangerous person who is to be feared in the community	The community is scared of him
Mqabuli (the kisser)	The name-bearer wanted to be perceived as someone who can get any woman he wants	The name-bearer is ridiculed because he is ugly and mentally handicapped
Nkalakatha (a streetwise person)	A fashionable and stylish young man	Perceived as a loafer
Mathufela (the pouting one)	Someone who is unkind	He is perceived as cold and not easy to get along with
Gigigi (throbbing sound of footprints)	Someone who has a great impact	Someone who runs around

Hearing a person's name for the first time may project humorous connotations. This phenomenon may be frequent when hearing names in other languages, as in the isiXhosa boys' names Philile (we are alive) or Thandekile (the loved one). These might be humorous to an isiZulu-speaking person because in the Zulu anthroponymicon *-ile* is a suffix for names given to girls. However, Brennen (2000: 141) argues that, over time, such a name loses its ability to raise even a smile: 'The urge to smile at the holder of the name because of the name fades, and after repeated exposure the name is no longer processed semantically' (2000: 141).

Projected connotations are closely linked with the expectations of the parents. By receiving a name, the individual implicitly accepts membership of the society and agrees to follow its rules and customs. For example, a person by the name of Gcinabazali (taking care of the parents) is expected to look after his parents when they become old. Sibani (light) is expected to bring light to difficult situations that the family is faced with. A boy by the name of Qedusizi (putting an end to poverty) is believed to be the one who will give his family a better life when he grows up. Names may express a whole way of life, as in the name Hlalezwini (staying in the Word); religious practices, as in the name Mnikelo (an offering); social systems, as in the name Hlalisile (staying with them); and cultural traditions, as in the name Nomsebenzi (mother of ancestral rituals).

Naming of an individual is a necessary step towards unifying the group. Without identity, an individual as well as the group would have no substance. The name is used to introduce the newborn to his or her ancestors during the *imbeleko* ceremony. This is carried out ten days after the baby is born to introduce the child to the ancestors. If a person dies, there are also rituals that must be performed for them to pass over to ancestorhood.

Cognitive content of a name
Hélène Jousse (2004) suggests that people who use the oral style have more practised memories. In KwaMambulu, people used their cognitive powers to remember what a person might have done in the past and still refer to that incident in the naming of their children. They rely solely on their memories to name children, referring to incidents that occurred

before they were born. For example, Qamndile (the talkative one), is a name given to a girl by her paternal grandmother because her mother was ostracised by her co-wives (before the girl was born) as a result of the fact that the mother of the child could not conceive and they were always talking about her.

Names as links to sociological phenomena

A name gives the name-bearer an identity and a position in a particular society. Names give the name-bearer a claim to what Mbiti calls 'the traditional solidarity in which the individual says: "I am because we are, and since we are, therefore I am"' (1969: 219). The name-bearer becomes known by that which they are called. Names deter confrontation within a family; they may, however, aggravate the friction by airing the conflict in public. The only advantage is that family members have retaliatory rights with regard to naming. For instance, a girl was given the name Bukani (what are you looking at?) by one co-wife, because she felt that her co-wives were always looking at her jealously. One of the co-wives gave birth to a baby girl and she named her Nginakenani (why do you worry yourself about what I do?) as a response to the name Bukani.

From the time a child is born, they are introduced to their living-dead by their personal name. The living-dead are informed of the arrival and are told to protect the child from evil spirits and jealous people. After the ceremony of *imbeleko*, the living-dead recognise this child because of its name. They act as guardian angels to protect this child. When a sorcerer wants to bewitch a person, the sorcerer calls out the name of that person. The name-bearer is affected wherever they are because a name forms part of their identity.

Names function not only as markers of personal identity, but they also index sociological structure. In other words, personal names are associated with individual uniqueness as well as with various elements of the social and cultural environments in which they are embedded (Miller 1927). Names form part of dynamic linguistic systems used by real people in real space and time. They possess what has been variously termed 'onomastic meaning', 'connotative meaning' (Nicolaisen 1976), 'associative meaning' (Grant 2006) and 'descriptive backing' (Searle 1969). These expressions bring to light the fact that names are more meaningful in the context within which they are used. 'Context' refers to factors such as, but certainly not limited to, the time and place of the speech act; the identities and personal histories of the participants involved in the speech act; the relations between participants (as in the name gender, kinship, status) and the situation (social and cultural) in which a speech act occurs (Strawson 1950).

Personal names are not the only way to vent people's frustrations. Animal names (such as for dogs) can also be used to articulate discontent and to air concerns about a situation. In KwaMambulu the following dog names reflect this practice: Bawuphethe (they really have it), Muthi (dangerous medicine), Jingane (monotony, persistence) and Basiphatheleni (what are they bringing for us?).

Homestead names also function as message conveyers in Zulu society. Mbali Shabalala discusses the way in which homestead names are used to reflect social dynamics in the Mabengela community in the Nkandla district of KwaZulu-Natal:

> From the study of Zulu homestead names in the Mabengela community and relevant field work, it was noticed that homestead names do not only refer to a particular homestead or distinguish it from others, but also reflect the social dynamics of the community of Mabengela. These names are given because of different circumstances affecting the family or the head of the family at a particular time. Homestead names are therefore never chosen without careful consideration of events surrounding the family, the clan or the society at large, they then are not just labels given at random (Shabalala 1999: 125).

Names and language links

There is a close relationship between the society and a language in which names are found. Names form an important part of a language, as William Nicolaisen notes: 'The acquisition of a language, another human trait, has given him [man] the tool with which to name' (1976).

Mbali Machaba asserts: 'Although names are found in a language, they do not only function as linguistic items. The fact that naming is not simply a linguistic matter, but a social and a psychological matter, is demonstrated by various naming practices adopted by people from different cultural and religious backgrounds' (2005: 29). In the case of names within polygynous families, names are used as channels of communication.

5

The Articulation of Conflict in Zulu Anthroponyms

The anthroponyms discussed in this chapter are used to alleviate feelings of tension and discontent towards people and/or situations. They indirectly comment on the behaviour of those in close relationships with the name-giver. More often than not this results from strained relationships between co-wives in polygynous households.

According to Noleen Turner: 'Oblique allusion is typical in the speech of most Zulu people. Allusive language is characteristic of various forms of Zulu oral traditions' (2003: 68). Similarly, while investigating the Scottish highlands, Nancy Dorian (1970) encountered a practice where nicknames are used to shun bad behaviour. She asserts: 'The actual use of such names, however, demands social competence in order to evaluate the offensiveness of such names – to a knowledge of social structure which is only available to "insiders".' Turner found something similar in her research in a Zulu setting: 'Out group members may be ignorant of the very existence of these names in most cases; moreover even when the "out group" members do know of their alternate names, they are most often totally unaware of any emotive or figurative underpinning that may be connected with these names' (2003: 69).

Names are used as a processual paradigm to maintain order in a traditional society. After a time, these names become obscure. This obscurity, according to Turner (2003), results from the use of metaphor and language, which are bound to a particular time and context. In the orality-literacy debate, Walter Ong coined the term 'oral residue' (1977: 13). KwaMambulu has a 'living' oral tradition, which means that the community displays a higher degree of residual orality.

African names serve the purpose of letting people know about situations taking place within families and the community at large.

These names give people an opportunity to vent their anger and voice their dissatisfaction, as in the name Zibeleni (why are you ignoring me?). It is also an opportunity for people to express their disappointment, as in Bajabhile (they are disappointed); their discontent with the world, as in naming the child Zwelinjani (what kind of world do we live in?); and their suspicions about people practising witchcraft, by giving a child the name Bhekumuthi (watching the use of *umuthi*).

These examples indicate that names are effective channels of communication. Turner (2003) analyses the strategies used by Zulu people, particularly in oral discourse (*izibongo*, or praise songs, and naming practices), and the way they articulate their frustrations and discontent in various social settings. She uses discourse analysis, which she believes 'treats the social environment as a "text" or rather a system of "texts" which can be analysed'. She describes the discourse as language usage in real contexts and argues:

> The articulation of disputes or conflicts in social environments occurs in the context of condensed or extended family settings, in the context of the neighbourhood or in a combination of family and neighbourhood. As important as the *function* of conflict articulation is the *form* that these oral expressions take amongst the Zulu (Turner 2003: 5; original emphasis).

Jack Mapanje and Landeg White (1983) document how different countries in Africa use songs as a form of expression. Songs are also used in the political arena throughout Africa to voice citizens' dissatisfaction and to directly address the injustices they face in their daily lives. These oral expressions are also used as pedagogical tools to shape social behaviour among the Haya community in Tanzania (Mutembei and Lugalla 2002). They are used with the intention of curbing unacceptable behaviour of community members. Ruth Finnegan mentions the use of oral 'poetry' and song in Africa for the expression and resolution of hostilities between individuals or groups in social settings, as well as in the political arena. Furthermore, Finnegan posits:

> Expression in poetry takes the sting out of the communication and removes it from the 'real' social arena. And yet, of course,

> it does not – for the communication still takes place. It is a curious example of the conventions that surround various forms of communication in society, where, even if the covert 'content' remains the same, the form radically affects the way it is received – whether or not it is regarded as a confrontation, for example (1970: 222).

In this way, Zulu names are sometimes regarded as a confrontation by the wrongdoer, who may in some cases feel compelled to respond.

Confrontation within polygynous families

Michael Lambert (2000) makes a comparison between African cultures as 'shame' cultures in contrast to 'guilt' cultures of the modern West. The difference, he maintains, is that shame cultures rely on external sanctions for good behaviour, while guilt cultures rely on the internalised conviction of sin. He further mentions that shame is a reaction to other people's criticism and that shame cultures are highly receptive to the disapproval of others. In a similar vein, Gabrielle Taylor claims: 'The distinguishing mark of a shame culture, and that which makes it different from a so-called guilt culture, is that here public esteem is the greatest good, and to be ill spoken of [is] the greatest evil' (in Turner 2003: 89).

Umsindo (noise), shouting, confrontation or disagreement is frowned upon in African societies. This kind of behaviour causes problems within the homestead and deeply angers the living-dead. It must be kept in mind that they are dead, but not gone. Therefore, all members of families, including co-wives, mothers-in-law and daughters-in-law must try to get along for the sake of the prosperity of the family. If a verbal confrontation starts between a mother-in-law and a daughter-in-law, the latter is usually sent to her father's house to fetch a goat or a cow that will be slaughtered to apologise to the living-dead.

African personal names may also involve implicit connotations. They may be indirect reactions to problematic situations in the lives of the name-bearers, their parents or their communities at large (Obeng 2001). Names are helpful tools for making the family and community know about the concerns and disappointments they may feel because of what the family members have done, as in the name Dumazigugu (being disappointed by the precious one). It is not always clear, as Samuel Gyasi Obeng points out, that the ambiguity involved in African naming traditions are the result of the restrictions placed on 'free' speech and the powerlessness of the name-givers. Turner explains:

> In Zulu society, the use of names, especially personal names (of people and animals), is an extremely useful channel of expressing discontent or passing criticism at those in close proximity, and is a vital way in which censure or tension is publicly aired, either with the intention of making others aware of the problem, or for the ultimate purpose of restraining or correcting an undesirable situation/behaviour trait, as direct confrontation or criticism is not an acceptable or preferred form of behaviour (1992: 45).

Names may not be specific to the person they are directed to, but they still serve the purpose of vocalising what is on the inside. Turner further argues: 'Names reflecting censure, disapproval and discontent serve an important social function in that they tend to minimize friction in the communal environment, by enabling a person about whom defamatory allegations have been made, to refute these accusations and attempt to clear his/her name in a subtle yet effective manner' (1992: 45).

The main purpose of this chapter is to discuss the underlying reasons for why people bestow the names they do on their children, and how names reflect social dynamics in the families within which they are found. It focuses mainly on the sociological aspects of names and naming practices: the names reflect social behaviours, which result from certain socialisation patterns. As Richard T. Schaefer and Robert P. Lamm, talking about sociological perspectives, note: 'Our major goal of this perspective is to identify underlying, recurring patterns of and influences on social behaviour' (1992: 5).

Choosing a personal name

There are many reasons why African people bestow the names they do on their children. Among other things, names may reflect circumstances surrounding the birth of a child, commemorate the living-dead, or describe how the child looked at birth. There is always a reason why a particular name is chosen for a particular person. Henri Alexandre Junod argues that there are many ways of giving a child a name:

> Everyone who has studied a Bantu tribe knows that in olden times, there were definite rules about naming a child and that the name itself was, in many cases, a kind of proverb. A mother will often give her child a name like '*Vuloyi*', i.e., witchcraft, as a challenge to public opinion, showing that she defies the verdict of the witchdoctor (1927).

Names in Zulu society

There are names used in official identities, such as identity documents, driver's licences, certificates, and so on, and names used in unofficial settings. An example of the latter is *igama lasekhaya* (the name used at home), which is perceived by Zulu people as sacred and part of the name-bearer's identity. It may be used for witchcraft and is therefore subject to the name avoidance (*hlonipha*) rules. *Ukuhlonipha* is an Nguni concept of respect and part of the rules are that one must avoid the names of one's in-laws. This name fixes a person within society, through a number of social dynamics. *Igama lesilungu* (a Euro-Western name) is a name that was (and still is) used mainly at school.

Some parents give English semantic extensions to the Zulu names they bestow on their children, with both names meaning the same thing – for example, Sbusiso Blessing, Jabulile Gladness, Sipho Gift and Moyomusha Freshness. Euro-Western names are not considered as a part of the person and are not subject to name avoidance (*hlonipha*) rules. *Isibongo* (surname) is the last name, which refers to the clan the bearer belongs to – for example, Zungu, Ngidi, Mtshali, Shange, Chamane and Gumede. Some examples of unofficial identities are *izithakazelo* (clan praise names), which are used to appeal to the person being addressed. To call Mr Zungu 'Manzini' is to affirm his identity within the wider socio-historical context, as is being addressed as Gwabini! Geda! Hamashe! Nyamakayishi isha ngabaphephezeli! or Somadise for a person of the Zungu clan.

It is common in Zulu society for a married couple to address each other by their first child's name. Teknonyms are not exclusively used by the couple, but also by the extended family and the community at large – for example, Baba kaNgenzeni (Ngenzeni's father) or Mama kaZibuyile (Zibuyile's mother). Patronyms (part of a personal name based on the given name of father, grandfather or an earlier male ancestor) have always been part of Zulu culture and identity – for example, in the names of Zulu kings, such as uSenzangakhona kaJama, (Senzangakhona, son of Jama) uCetshwayo kaMpande (Cetshwayo, son of Mpande). In Zulu society, a patronym can also be also used to address married women as a term of endearment (by prefixing Ma – mother of – to the woman's father's name) – for example, UMaFakazi Ngidi being addressed as uMaSkali (daughter of Skali) and MaHlongwa Ngidi being addressed as MaSthende (daughter of Sthende). They are also used to address women whose fathers have English names – for example, MaNgubane Ngidi being addressed as MaTomseni (daughter of Thompson, which is phonologised into isiZulu as Tomseni).

Proverbial names criticise, admonish, praise or explain a course of action by a member or members of the community and are used as strategic alternatives to confrontational discourse. Examples of such names include: Mahlomeka (Mr Doesn't-think-before-he-acts), Mudemude (Mr Tall one) and Mshin'ozishintshayo (Mr Automatic machine gun) for someone who is good at soccer. This is a common trend in most African societies. The indirectness involved in the creation of proverbial names is motivated by the fact that in African societies, indirectness is an acceptable and a comprehensible mode of communication. Expressing one's feeling indirectly is therefore not considered a deliberate attempt by the speaker to be vague, or to be an act of insincerity.

There are many names that people use to send the message to others. For instance, a woman who believed that her co-wives were always interested in her affairs and enquiring about her state named her son Buzelukwenzani (this does not concern you, so what do you want to know). Obeng states:

> Proverbial names could be invoked to respond to social stimuli. Thus, a man who has named his son Mpemeawu 'if you don't like me, die' i.e. 'to hell with you' might call or mention the

name of his son when he overhears people gossiping about how they dislike him. In such a context, the proverbial names situate meaning in that particular communicative context (2001: 51–2).

Many onomasticians argue that names are more meaningful in the context within which they are used. The data collected for the purposes of this book shows that names are a means of communication that mostly benefits the name-giver. The name-giver gets the opportunity to express themself in the name. For instance, giving a child a name like Bangifunani (what do they want from me?) is, in this instance, to the benefit of the mother who gave her daughter this name to act as a defence mechanism against her co-wives' bad treatment. In the context of a polygynous family, such a name might deter an argument that could spiral out of control, which would be detrimental to the harmonious living within the homestead. Names outlive the name-givers in most cases. This poses a challenge in situations where the grievances were addressed and people reconciled, and yet the name still acts as a constant reminder of what once was. Furthermore, the children are then stuck with names that reflect a conflict about which they know very little.

A polygynous context informs the conflict between family members. The society 'subconsciously' expects polygynous families to have conflict, to the extent that if a man has two wives who are not fighting, there is an assumption that it is because the husband used *umuthi* to make his wives submit to him (*ukuhlanganisa abafazi*). This assumption causes people within this context to think that their behaviour is always justified. The society condones any kind of exchange of unpleasant words because within a polygynous context the person who is perceived as the wrongdoer can always retaliate, either by giving a name that is a direct response or a question on the prospective name. This way of communicating is effective in the sense that as long as there are children being born, the 'wrongdoer' can defend themself. This objectifies the name-bearer as the name given makes the name-bearer a tool with which to fight the enemy, as in the name Mdindeni (beat him up), a shield for protection; the name Sphephelo (the refuge); or a loudspeaker to announce foul play, as in the name Hletshiwe (the one they gossip about). There is no consideration for the feelings of the name-bearers. When the name-bearer grows up, it is up to them to decide either to keep, discard or shorten the name.

It is important to note here that living conditions are not always unstable in polygamous families. There are a few reported cases where everything seems all right – for example, if the first wife chose the second wife and they end up being friends, rather than rivals. However, nowadays, this is not as common as it used to be. Problems are usually prominent in traditional polygamous families, where a husband might have three wives from different social upbringings, for example. In such cases, the use of love potions is suspected because each wife is fighting for her husband's attention and affection.

Categories of personal names

In this book, the data is divided into different categories. These categories reflect the dynamics within the living conditions of the polygynous families in KwaMambulu. These dynamics are about the social lives of family members and their relationships with each other.

Names that reflect love and hatred

Thandwangubani (who is going to love him?)
This boy was named by his mother. His father did not want anything to do with his pregnant mother.

Zondani (what is it you hate about me?)
The mother was asking this of her co-wives, who hated her for no apparent reason.

Hlanyukiwe (the deserted one)
While the mother was pregnant, everybody, including her husband, deserted her. She then gave this name to her daughter to let everybody know how she felt.

Bhekubala (watching nothing)
The mother was asking what the father was watching when he allowed her rivals to do whatever they wanted to her in his presence.

Names that reflect gossip

Having women sharing a husband in one homestead may sometimes be asking too much of the husband. It sometimes becomes impossible for him to satisfy all of them. This becomes apparent when there is a disagreement between co-wives: the husband is caught in the middle. He is always in a predicament because in his wives' eyes he can never be completely impartial. The co-wives are constantly on the lookout as far as their husband's behaviour is concerned. There are usually allegations that he favours a certain wife over others. Co-wives often gang up on the favourite wife and scrutinise her behaviour and conduct.

Bachazani (what do they mean?)
The mother, who was the name-giver, was asking her sisters-in-law about the bad things they always said about her behind her back.

Thangithini (what do you want me to say?)
The father, who gave this name to the child, did not know what to say when his wife was always complaining about her co-wives who were gossiping about her.

Mhletshwa (the one they gossip about)
The co-wives were always gossiping about the mother of this child. He was given this name by his mother, with the hope that they would stop talking about her.

Hlushwayini (what is bothering you?)
The mother of this child wanted to know what was bothering her rivals when they made it their mission to destroy her by lying about her.

Ncengutshwala (begging for liquor)
One of the co-wives, who was a drunkard, always talked about the mother of this child when people offered her liquor. The mother felt that she had to point that out.

Ndabiyesinda (a heavy/difficult issue)
It was difficult for the mother of this girl because everybody gossiped about her and made up stories. She gave this name to her baby girl to let her feelings be known.

Tshenwephi (where did you get that information from?)
There was a lot of gossip going on about the mother of this child and she wondered from where the people got their facts. The mother of this child gave her this name.

Khohlwayezakhe (he/she forgets his/her own affairs)
The mother's co-wives did not want to talk about their affairs in public, but were more than eager to privately discuss other people's affairs. The mother gave this name to her baby boy to stop them from talking about her.

Bahlekabonke (they are all smiling)
The mother of this child named him after she had learnt the hard way that even when people hate you, and say bad things about you behind your back, they still smile at you and pretend to be your friends.

Names that reflect jealousy

Jealousy is at the root of most if not all problems in polygamous marriages. S. Dwane notes: 'Men may not easily appreciate that it costs a woman to share her husband and the father of her children with several wives' (1975: 235–6). Furthermore, when wives of a polygynist compete, 'this is frequently not a manifestation of petty jealousies but a loud reminder that there is something wrong that needs to be attended to'.

It becomes a problem in a polygynous family when everything becomes competitive among family members. Mushir Hosain Kidwai argues why polygamy is not ideal:

> We all agree that polygamy is not a first-class institution, because it disturbs the society by creating mutual jealousy between two wives of the same man. And this jealousy is due to the fact that one husband cannot be equitable between his two wives... A Muslim is permitted to marry more than one wife, but on condition that all the wives should be equally treated, and no room should be left for injustice or inequity, and no occasion given for mutual jealousy (n.d.: 5–7).

The following are names that refer to jealousy.

Bancamile (they have not succeeded)
For quite a while, the mother of this child could not fall pregnant, but her husband stood by her. Her in-laws then alleged that she could not fall pregnant because of a snake called *umaMlambo* (a magical love potion that causes barrenness to the keeper of the snake, but makes the husband love her more). But at last she fell pregnant and it was proved that their allegations were wrong and she gave this name to her daughter.

Vimbephi (where am I stopping you?)
The mother of this child gave her this name as a result of her co-wives being jealous of her because her husband loved her. She thought they too could get the same attention from the husband if he wanted to, because she never did anything to stop him from visiting them. It was his choice to spend more time with her.

Bajabhile (they were disappointed)
The co-wives were jealous because their husband loved the mother of this child more than he loved them. They started to say nasty things about her, hoping that the husband would leave her, and much to their surprise he did not. She gave the girl this name to say they could not stop what was happening.

Names that reflect witchcraft
Quarrels and fights among the wives and children sometimes occur because of favouritism. The husband may neglect some wives because he favours others. This sometimes leads to accusation of witchcraft, as John Mbiti infers:

> Sometimes feelings of jealousy may lead to practicing witchcraft. If one of the co-wives feels slighted or mistreated, she may seek the service of a witchdoctor, who is believed to be able to cast a spell upon a co-wife, her children or even upon a husband. Witchcraft is one of the most feared and hated phenomena in many African societies; one which can lead to dissolution of a marriage (1969: 200).

Mothers, and sometimes fathers, voice these issues in the naming process. The women may become jealous of one another and end up practising witchcraft. They sometimes go to diviners (*izangoma*) who will confirm that there is something wrong within the family set-up. It is up to the person who went to the diviner to figure out who the culprit is, as the diviner never gives names, only clues. John H. Beattie comments on the Nyoro naming system:

> A victim may, however, indicate more subtly his opinion that somebody (and he may or may not suspect who that person is) is working against him, and the Nyoro system of personal nomenclature provides one way of doing this ... And if his tormentors conclude that their victim has recognized them, and may, who knows, be planning retaliatory actions, they may think it is wise to leave him alone (1957: 106).

The following are examples of names in this category.

Buyelaphi (where do you come back to?)
This woman's older child was coming home after spending six months at a herbalist's home because she was ill and the mother was wondering if it was safe for her to return. She gave this name to her newborn daughter.

Mzonzima (a difficult home to live in)
This child was given this name by her paternal grandmother because when everybody uses *umuthi* or witchcraft to fight their battles and settle their personal scores, it is difficult to live in such an environment.

Khulelaphi (where are you going to grow up?)
There were sorcerers within the homestead and because of this the mother of this child was worried about the welfare of her children and gave the child this name.

Bulewephi (where was she bewitched?)
The mother of this child alleged that her co-wives bewitched her while she was pregnant, but the husband doubted that his wives could do such

a thing. In response, the mother asked sarcastically where she and her older child were bewitched by giving this name to her third daughter.

Fikelephi (where did she arrive at?)
This mother was happy that she had a daughter, but was afraid of the sorcerers around the homestead. She gave this name, which is a plea to her daughter, as she wondered about the deadly circumstances she was born into.

Khawulani (you must stop)
The mother was tired of people bewitching her, so she was telling them to stop by giving this name to her last-born boy.

Zotholani (what are you going to achieve?)
This name was given by the father of a child who was angry with his wife because she alleged that her co-wives were bewitching her, and he did not believe this was true. In another instance, the mother gave this name to her daughter, as she was asking her in-laws about what they were going to achieve by bewitching her.

Nyathelephi (what did she step on?)
This name was given by a grandmother who wanted to know the origins of her granddaughter's illness. The grandmother believed that the girl born before Nyathelephi must have stumbled over *umuthi* and fallen ill.

Mzungezeni (surround him)
This father was asking his living-dead to surround (protect) his son, so that he could not be seen by enemies.

Bhekamuphi (which one should I watch?)
In giving her son this name, this mother was levelling an accusation at her co-wives of practising witchcraft. She was not sure which one was the culprit and therefore asks the question in the name about which one to guard against.

Names that reflect quarrels over inheritance

Fights over inheritance start long before the husband dies. In Zulu culture, the first wife's (*indlunkulu*) firstborn son (*inkosana*) is the one who inherits everything and takes over from his father as the head of the homestead. These days, like everything, culture has evolved. The fact that your mother married first and that you were born before everybody else does not mean that you have more rights than everybody else to your father's inheritance, and that your half-brothers will go empty-handed. This is clearly indicated in the following examples.

Mbangiseni (what are you fighting with him for?)
Everybody knew that the mother of this child, as the first wife, would give birth to the heir; as soon as that happened, her co-wives could not accept it and wanted their share. The co-wives thought that their children should have a share in the husband's estate even before this boy was born. When the mother gave birth to the boy, she gave him this name.

Nkosiyombango (king of disputes)
The mother of this boy felt that although there were disputes about who was going to inherit, this child was the rightful heir and she gave him this name to reiterate her point.

Bhekamafa (pining over other people's inheritances)
One of the co-wives always wanted to get something when people died. The mother of this boy wanted the whole community to know about her co-wife's behaviour.

Gcinangokubusa (end up by living a good life)
The mother of this child felt that even though there were disputes about the fact that her child was the rightful one to inherit everything when the father died, in the end, everyone would have no choice but to accept this and he would end up living a good life.

Gqibokwakhe (hiding her possessions)
The second wife was hiding what she had inherited from her family to try to extort belongings from her husband's family. The mother of this

boy wanted to let everyone know that this co-wife came from an affluent family, but she wanted to hide it. This name was given to the boy by his grandmother, who wanted to point out that his mother was stingy and selfish.

Gcinokwakhe (keeping her own possessions)
The mother of this boy implied that she was going to keep her own things; as the second wife, she knew that she would not inherit anything from her husband.

Bangifa (fighting over inheritance)
This child was born immediately after his father had passed away, at which time everybody was fighting over who was to get what from the inheritance. His mother was the one who gave him the name.

Ngenzeleni (what have you done for me?)
The husband had never done anything for the mother of this child when he was alive; when he died, everything went to the heir (the first wife's son). She was furious and gave her girl this name.

Names that reflect that the husband cannot provide for everybody
Because of the number of wives each man takes, it is sometimes difficult for him to provide for everybody in the same way and keep everybody happy. The following are examples of names in this category.

Dlezakhe (eating his/her own)
The mother of this boy and her children survived only through her parents. Her husband never gave her anything; he was always 'eating' his own money with the wives he preferred. She gave the child this name to point out the husband's bad behaviour.

Bongathini (what should I say in thanking you?)
The mother of this child gave her this name because she wanted to know what she should be thankful and grateful for since her husband could not provide for them.

Ngizomphani (what am I going to feed her?)
The mother of this child had no idea what to feed her child as she had no job and her husband gave them nothing. She gave the child this name as an expression of her thoughts and concerns.

Names that reflect favouritism
It must be noted that there is a lot of favouritism within polygamous families. This is understandable, considering that the husband is faced with, for example, three different women who are equally beautiful and he must choose one over the others. He cannot help but be confused at times.

Mzwangedwa (loneliness)
The mother of this child gave this name to him as she felt lonely all the time because she was not the favourite wife and her husband rarely visited her.

Zibelani (why are you ignoring me?)
The mother of this child felt ignored by her husband and gave the name to her son to make her husband aware of the situation.

Ntombizaphi (where are these girls from?)
The mother of this girl wanted to know where her co-wives came from because they received better treatment from the husband, and so she gave this name to her baby girl.

Names that reflect promiscuity
When the wives are given no attention while the husband is entertaining the latest addition to his 'wife collection', the wives are left with no choice but to find attention elsewhere.

Buzakunyoko (ask your mother)
The father of this child suspected that his wife had been unfaithful to him and assumed that the child was not his. He gave him this name so that when his child grew up and wanted to know his father and his real surname, he would be able to detect from the very name as to whom he could get the answers from.

Names that reflect lack of intimacy
It must be remembered that the husband takes turns in 'visiting' his wives. Therefore, each wife waits three to four days (depending on the number of wives the husband has) before being intimate with her husband.

Sibangaliphi (which one [penis] are we fighting over?)
The mother of the child bestowed this name on her son because the co-wives were bitter towards each other when the man of the homestead had 'temporary' erectile dysfunction. The word 'penis' is not in the name itself but is implied using *li-* (it) for *ipipi* (penis), which is a noun class 5 concord.

Nakwawubani (who is going to pay attention to me?)
As extramarital affairs for married women are unheard of, the mother of this child wondered from where she would get sexual attention since her husband was not giving her any. She then gave this name to her son to make her concerns known.

Ngoneni (what have I done wrong?)
The mother of this girl wanted to know what she had done wrong for her husband to reject her and not want to be intimate with her.

Zokwenzani (what am I going to do?)
The mother of this girl was not sure what steps to take to get her husband's attention with regard to her sexual needs.

Veluyeke (just stop doing it if you don't want to)
One boy got this name because his mother was not happy with the amount of attention she was getting from her husband. In another instance, the mother was not satisfied with the 'sexual performance' of her husband and gave her child this name to alert him to her concerns.

Names that allege that the children are illegitimate
Because of the number of wives, and the fact that it takes time for the husband to be intimate with each of them, it sometimes becomes

impossible for them to fall pregnant. In cases where the husband works in town and only comes home a few times a year, it raises concern when he finds one of his wives pregnant. In this category, a mother may give a sarcastic name to the child to show the father that she is aware that he does not believe the child is his.

Muntukabani (whose child is this?)
The name was given by a mother in response to the father's allegations about her being unfaithful and him not being the father.

Fikanaye (arriving with him)
The name was given by the father after suspecting that his wife might have been already pregnant when they met.

Qhamukephi (where did she come from?)
The father of this child was said to be away in Johannesburg working when the child was conceived, so the grandmother, who bestowed the name, wanted to know where she came from, implying that her daughter-in-law was unfaithful to her son.

Qapheleni (what are you watching?)
The grandmother who gave this name was asking her son (the father of the child) as to what he was watching if his wife could have had an affair right under his nose.

Bazothini (what are people going to say?)
The father gave this name to his daughter because he wanted to know what the people would say when they find out that the child was illegitimate.

Names that reflect conflict
Conflict within a polygamous family can be caused by anything. Sometimes it is caused by the rules laid down by the head of the homestead, and he may be biased in as far as the application of those rules is concerned. The harshness, leniency or fairness in the application of the rules depends on the wife he prefers.

Mthethokayizwani (rules are conflicting)
This boy was given the name by his father because everyone within the homestead was making their own rules and doing as they pleased because the wives had lost respect for their husband. He was not fair and that was where the controversy started.

Bhekimthetho (making sure the rules are followed)
One of the wives appointed herself to the position of being her husband's assistant. She would tell her co-wives what to do and what not to do. The mother of this boy gave him the name to ridicule the co-wife concerned.

Phumasilwe (go out and fight me)
The co-wife was always saying to the mother of this child: '*Phuma uze lana ngikushaye*' (Come out here so I may hit you) or '*Phumela phandle silwe*' (Come outside so we may fight), thus the mother gave her child this name.

Hlalempini (living in the war zone)
The father gave this name to his son because there was always fighting in his homestead; wives were fighting each other and their children were following suit. He then felt that the situation was unbearable and that he lived on a battlefield.

Muziwenduku (house of fighting)
This name was given by a mother to a child whose father believed that in order to solve problems he had to hit his wives.

Fundakubona (learned from them)
The mother gave this name to her child to dispute allegations that she was always causing trouble and fights within the homestead. She claimed that she learnt from the same people making the allegations.

Moyomusha (fresh air)
The father gave the name to his baby girl after he got married to her mother because he was no longer happy with his elder wife, who was always fighting with him, so instead he wanted some fresh air.

Names suggesting that co-wives are using love potions on their husband

Women who feel unloved and get no attention from their husbands often feel obliged to use love potions to make their husbands fall in love with them again. Some might argue that these women should just leave the man, instead of taking such drastic steps to force somebody to love them.

Ntandoni (what kind of a love potion is it?)
This name was given by the mother of this child because of the allegation that one of the co-wives was using a strong love potion, which caused her husband to reject his other wives.

Fumbetheni (what do you have in your hand?)
The mother of this child gave this name after suspecting that her co-wife was using a love potion on their husband.

Names that reflect the fact that the wife has accepted that she is not good enough for her husband

Being in daily competition causes some of these women to lose confidence in themselves and to have low self-esteem. They come to a point where they accept their predicament and just continue with their lives.

Zokwenzani (what am I going to do?)
The mother of this child did not know what to do with the fact that her husband thought she was not good enough.

Thembokwakhe (trusting her own)
The mother of this child had learnt to trust nobody and to be self-sufficient where her family was concerned.

Simethembeni (why do we trust him?)
The mother of this boy was blaming herself for trusting her husband who was never there for her.

Melwawubani (who is going to speak on my behalf?)
This woman felt that her husband did not support her in her ventures. She gave this name to her daughter with an expectation that the husband was going to change.

Nhlalayenza (it is my daily bread)
The mother of this boy was used to being treated as nothing that mattered.

Khohlwangifile (I'll die before I forget)
The mother of this child said her son's name was an indication of the rejection and the suffering she experienced while nobody was paying attention to her.

Conclusion

Zulu people have various reasons for bestowing the kinds of names they do on their children. Behind every African name is a story, but whether the name-bearer is willing to share the story is a different matter altogether. Most people are not comfortable with disclosing their domestic squabbles to the whole community. Names discussed in this chapter are just a reflection of how tough life can be in some polygynous homesteads. These names, however, are of crucial importance as they deter confrontation, which would lead to people yelling at each other and even fighting. This would anger their living-dead – something every African person avoids at all costs because the price paid for irritating the living-dead is very high. They even avoid the names of their in-laws for fear of the unknown – nobody really knows for sure what happens when a bride says her father-in-law's name and nobody is willing to take the risk to find out. They might not live to tell the tale. If the elders say it should not be done, it should not be done. That might also act as a deterrent to stop people from wanting to know what would happen to them and their families if they did the forbidden. S.M. Suzman puts it this way: 'Name-giving provides an outlet for the regulation of social relations in the intense social interaction of small communities. It allows people to communicate their feelings indirectly, without overt confrontation and possible conflict' (1994: 270).

The naming process becomes a constant reminder of a pre-existing war of words between parents. These names stir up conflict that could have subsided in the next generation. About 30 per cent of the families I interviewed in KwaMambulu are not on speaking terms with other members of the same family, over conflict for reasons they are not sure of. They grew up with the resentment, they inherited it from their parents and they pass it on to their children. The conflict outlives its own cause and only dies when those who knew about it die.

6

Penthonyms as Reflections of Social Behaviour Patterns

Penthonyms (names that express cultural attitudes towards the death of relatives, such as sorrow and mourning) are perceived as contextual variations used as communication strategies in oral communities. They are used as vehicles for transporting messages to the intended recipient while avoiding confrontation, as Ruth Finnegan (1970) argues is common across Africa. These anthroponyms are aimed at diffusing direct conflict by indirectly articulating issues of conflict in a family context.

Allegations of the practice of witchcraft and sorcery are always alluded to in Zulu society when death strikes. When parents suffer the misfortune of losing children, they bestow names that are directed to (1) death itself; (2) to sorcerers who are thought to be bewitching the child; or (3) to the evil spirits who are believed to be making the child weaker. Some names may seem negative and wish ill-health to the name-bearer, but in fact they are intended to deceive the evil spirits to leave the child alone by making them think that the child is not wanted by the parents. These names are given to male children because they are the ones who continue the family name.

Names in Zulu culture result from circumstances surrounding the conception, pregnancy and the birth of a child. Bestowing a name on an individual is a religious practice. S.M.E. Bhengu states:

> A traditional African name is a religious mark of personal and human identification. It is a symbol of honour and respect for the physical environment in which human experience flourishes positively or negatively. The community uses names as an instrument to build and mould the character of the younger, to

fortify that of the adult, and to reward that of the elder (1975: 52).

Names in African cultures are pointers to the name-givers' hopes, dreams and aspirations. They may reflect their geographical environments, their fears (Nokudinga, mother of loitering), their religious beliefs (Nomkhuleko, mother of prayer) or their philosophy of life and death (Nomadlozi, mother of ancestral spirits). Children's names may even provide insights into important cultural or sociopolitical events at the time of their birth (Mpisendlini, the battle is in the house). The circumstances surrounding a child's birth may be considered when a name is being chosen. Factors such as the day of the week (Nomgqibelo, mother of Saturdays, or Nomasonto, mother of Sundays); the time of day (Nokusa, mother of dawn, or Khwezi, star of the dawn); morning, dusk, afternoon (Minenhle, good day); evening, night (Nobusuku, mother of the night); the season of the year (Langalibalele, the sun is shining); the order of birth (Mafungwase, firstborn girl; Mfanafuthi, boy again; or Ntombintathu, three girls one after another) may influence the name given to a child. Other factors include where a person is born (Nonkantolo, mother of the courts); the specific circumstances relating to the child and to the child's family (Zophiwani, what are we going to feed him/her); the attitude of the parents (Siyathokoza, we are happy, or Bancamile, they are disappointed), as well as the gender of the child (Ntombi, young maiden or Nsizwa, young man). All of these factors play significant roles in the overall naming process and in the actual name given.

Death-prevention names
Survival names reflect sociological issues, family dynamics, ancestral wrath and attack by evil spirits. In most African societies, survival names are seen as death-preventing, but in Zulu culture they are mainly directed at evil spirits in order to prevent death and emphasise the survival of the child. Survival names are names given to children so that they can survive childhood diseases. They are thus death-prevention names and are given to the children of couples who may previously have suffered infant mortality. Samuel Gyasi Obeng argues: 'In giving children survival

names, the children's biological parents hope that even if the members of the spirit world recognise the children eventually, they will be so angry (because of the ugly nature of the survival name) that they will not call the child to the spirit world' (2001: 91). When talking about the Bhaca of the Eastern Cape, William Hammond-Tooke remarks: 'Informants state that parents are reluctant to give flattering names to children, "children who are given good names do not live", and one comes across such names as *Falinzima* (scarce inheritance), *Dingilizwe* (one-who-has-no-country) and *Mazubale* (one-who-faints)' (1974: 216).

Ancestors are put on a pedestal by most African cultures; they hold a high position in society. If people have issues with ancestors or something that has happened, and they believe it is the ancestors' fault, it is easy to channel that anger to a name they give to a child, as Obeng notes:

> Survival names and other related names may epitomise cultural ideas and values as well as the wishes of the society which gives them. Societies create such names to help deal with emotions associated with the loss of a loved one and grief associated with such a loss . . . the names are created to help members of the society to speak the unspeakable (2001: 94).

Thus, in Akan society it is considered rude to speak in a command form to the ancestors and the members of the spirit world because they have a higher status than the living. However, through survival names, name-givers can communicate with the ancestors in a command form, as evidenced by the verbs in the imperative mood.

H.O. Mönnig explains the concept of survival names:

> Families who have misfortune with previous children will treat a new child in a peculiar manner. Parents who have lost a few children will name a new-born daughter Mosa (son) while a son will be named Ngwanenyana (small daughter). They will also be clothed and treated as if they belong to the opposite sex. Mothers who have had a number of still-born children will give a child an unpleasant name. These children are treated as if they are unwanted. Their hair is dressed differently from other children,

and they are mostly avoided. This is done to confuse the ancestral spirits into thinking that the parents do not care for them, and that taking them away will not further punish the parents (cited in Koopman 1986: 28).

This is evident in most African societies. Parents do not give negative names to their children because they do not like the child, but because such names are a disguise for the affection they have for it. Ogonna Chuks-Orji argues that this love of the children is to be universally observed in the names the children bear:

> Thus, even the quite uncomplimentary name Chotsani 'take it away' (Yao, Malawi), is not, in fact, an expression of rejection but rather an attempt by the family to conceal or disguise its joy so that the divinities or the ancestors will not take back the precious infant.
> . . . the first name given may be quite uncomplimentary, for instance 'I am dead' or 'I am ugly'. In this way, it is hoped to avoid the jealousy of the ancestors who might wish to take back to themselves a child who is especially healthy or good looking (1972: 82).

If one's parents suffer or have suffered a child or infant mortality, a survival or death-prevention name is believed to be capable of preventing and/or totally eliminating such deaths since it has the power of preventing parents in the underworld from causing the death of such children – for example, Myekeni (leave him alone) and Mvikeleni (protect him). Names in African societies may even be important indicator(s) of the bearers' behaviour and act as pointers to the name-bearers' past, present and future accomplishments. There is also a close relationship between the name and the name-bearer since the name links the name-bearer to the name-giver's overall experiences.

The social significance of witchcraft
The subjects of witchcraft, sorcery and the incorrect way of using *umuthi* are sensitive subjects in Zulu society. Family members of the

name-bearers are not always willing to share their stories. During my fieldwork in KwaMambulu, I had to spend some time with the families I wanted to interview, so that family members became acquainted with me and trusted me before they provided background to some of the names.

Rolf Kuschel (1988) mentions that there is a strong connection between names and the sociocultural life of a people, given the growing recognition that social institutions do not develop or exist in a vacuum. Names, therefore, relate to other parts of a culture; they are marks of identity, solidarity and social cohesion. Names have a strong significance in people's beliefs in Zulu culture. According to Kofi Agyekum (2006), names are pointers to people's way of life and sociocultural experience and give deep insights into the cultural patterns, beliefs, ideology and religion of a people.

Names form an integral part of Zulu culture to give identity to the name-bearer. As Peter Sarpong (1974) rightly points out, one is not simply called X, one *is* X. Zulu society believes that sorcerers use people's names to bewitch them. Sorcerers may use people's names at night while using *umuthi* (traditional medicine) that will cause them to become sick. As a result, it is believed that there are many illnesses caused by sorcerers using people's names to bewitch them, as Axel-Ivar Berglund expatiates in the following interview:

> Our discussion continued in terms of the name of the person who was to be harmed.
>
> Berglund: 'Everywhere I am told that *umthakathi* [one who practises witchcraft] mentions the name of the person who is to be killed. Why does *umthakathi* mention the name?'
>
> 'It is the name of that person.'
>
> Berglund: 'Is it important that the name should be mentioned?'
>
> 'It is very important. It is the important thing in *ubuthakathi* [the act of witchcraft]. If a man can hide his name from people, then he can hide from much evil. *Umthakathi* can kill a man if he lacks vileness (body-dirt) and hair but has the name. So the name is very important.'
>
> Berglund: 'Why is the name of the person so important?'

'The name is that person. They are the same, the name and the person. It is the word whereby that person is known. That is the name. So, the person and the name are one. *Umthakathi* kills a man by combining the words of death with the name. He throws (*ukuphonsa*) these at the man and they kill him' (1976: 291).

In KwaMambulu, there were a number of names suggesting a belief in witchcraft, as in the names Felamandla (he is bewitched because he is strong), Bhekumuthi (watching the use of *umuthi*), Nyathelephi (where did you put your foot?) and Fumbetheni (what do you have in your closed hand?).

The African way of viewing death

The concept of death is a social, spiritual and religious phenomenon in most African societies. In Zulu society death is not believed to be the end of life but the beginning of the hereafter.

Ancestors are believed to have supernatural powers and there is always a need to venerate them. In a broader context, Gailyn van Rheenen (1991) remarks that the veneration of ancestors is deeply ingrained in the sociocultural and spiritual consciousness of the Ibibio people of Nigeria. He writes: 'This awareness is rooted in the belief that spiritual beings and forces have power over human affairs and that humans, consequently, must discover how these beings and forces are impacting on them in order to determine future action' (1991: 345). This is also true in the Zulu context. Sorcery and the use of witchcraft sometimes result in death. Zulu people use several expressions to describe death. These expressions are reflective of the way they perceive the state of the dead:

Akasekho (he is no more)
Usishiyile (he left us)
Ushonile (he went beneath)
Ufile (he died)
Uhambile (he left)

Uye ekhaya (he went home)
Udlulile (he passed on)
Wendile (used if a twin should die, from the verb *-enda*, to get married)

How African people view death and what happens thereafter is crucial to the way they behave in and around the homestead, in the way they conduct themselves when they have disagreements and in channelling their anger through the names they give to their children that show their discontent. The fact that African people perceive their dead relatives as playing a big role in their own lives keeps the living family members in line.

Survival names

Survival names reflect the emotions of the name-giver. They consider what and how the name-giver felt over the loss of the child. Samuel Gyasi Obeng remarks:

> The negative emotion chronicles painful experiences, frustration, and a sense of life dissatisfaction of the name-giver. Such names express self-pity, bitterness, depression and grief. They are products of the reaction these emotions provoke as a function of a culturally normative behaviour. The positive emotions, alternatively, primarily evoke a sense of hope with the belief that circumstances may change and turn out better. These names tend to console and inspire the namegiver/bearer regarding the existence of possibilities (2001: 94).

Obeng observes that among the Ibibio people of Nigeria, death-prevention names are psychological imperatives or antidotes that can maintain some level of assurance and security that is vital for a child's survival. He further argues:

> There are pragmatic motivations for the choice of death prevention names which can be broadly contextualised and understood in terms of the values and belief systems of the

Ibibio people. These names are mostly connotative and contain encyclopaedic information that reflects the worldview and cultural environment of the Ibibio people. This is because anyone who is not knowledgeable in the local communicative practice of the Ibibio cannot make any sense of the names (2001: 112).

Survival names are given to male children because they are believed to be the future of the family. They get married and father children to carry down the family name. The male children protect the family and when the man of the house dies the male children take over family matters.

In order to contextualise these names in the custom and tradition of Zulu society, this chapter adopts the functions of survival names listed in Obeng (2001: 69):

- to deceive the spiritual forces that the child is worthless since it has been given a despicable name by the biological parents – for example, Zibizendlela (rubbish of the pathway);
- to hide the identity of the name-bearer from the underworld forces – for example, Mkhohliseni (deceive him);
- to question the uncertainty and temporary nature of life – for example, Mchitheni (destroy him);
- to recognise the existence of superior powers or forces that hold the keys of life and death – for example, Philangenkosi (alive because of the Lord);
- to provide psychological relief to the name-giver for the tension generated by past frustrating experiences – for example, Sizophila (we will live); and
- to demonstrate invincibility – for example, Gadla (I dare you to attack).

Survival names are names given to children so that they can survive childhood diseases. They are thus death-prevention names and are given to the children of couples who may have previously suffered an infant mortality. Some of the survival names are bestowed in order to plead with the evil forces, sorcerers and death can be seen in the following examples:

- Mkhululeni (free him): The parents of this child had seen their children suffer from various ailments and die in infancy. When this child was born they were pleading with the evil spirits to free this child from suffering.
- Mchazeleni (explain to him): The parents of this child were pleading with evil spirits to explain why the child should suffer so much.
- Mxoleleni (forgive him): The parents felt that they were being punished for something by having their children taken in their infancy; they were asking the evil spirits to forgive the child and let the child live.
- Mphumuzeni (make him rest): The parents of this child were pleading with the dark forces to leave the child alone so that they (the parents) could rest and enjoy life.
- Myekeni (leave him): The parents were hoping that the evil spirits would leave the child alone, which would put an end to their suffering.

Obeng also mentions that 'some bearers of survival names are sometimes ridiculed by other people due to ignorance of others about the Akan culture. There is no doubt, however, that survival names communicate strong messages and are relevant to the name-bearers in particular and to the society at large' (2001: 76). This is also a problem in Zulu culture. The name-givers bestow these names to ask protection from the ancestors, as in the following examples:
- Mzungezeni (surround him): The parents were giving instructions to the ancestors to surround the child so that they are protected from the evil spirits.
- Mqiniseni (make him strong): This is a plea to the ancestors to protect the child, so it can survive.
- Mbuyiseni (bring him back): In Zulu society it is believed that when a person dies, they go to live with the ancestors, so the ancestors can bring back a near-death person by restoring good life.
- Mhlengeni (save him): This name is a plea for the ancestors to heal the child from ailments that can cause death.

- Mnikeni (give him chance): After suffering an infant mortality, the parents are asking the ancestors to give the child a chance to live.
- Mtshengiseni (show him): The parents are asking the ancestors to show the child the way to good health and a successful life.
- Mmiseni (stand with him): If the ancestors stand next to the child, that child will be protected and will not get sick or die.
- Mvikeleni (protect him): The child needs to be protected from the evil spirits.
- Mkhetheni (choose him among others): From all the children that have died, the parents plead with the ancestors to choose this child as the one who will escape death and live.
- Mfihleni (hide him): Protection by the ancestors is important in warding off the attacks of evil spirits.
- Mhlaliseni (stay with him): The parents strongly believe that if the ancestors stay with this child, it will be protected from any kind of attack.
- Mthandeni (love him): This sarcastic name is a plea to the evil spirits to love the child they are trying to kill and give it a chance to live.

If people have issues with ancestors or what has happened in their lives, and they believe it is due to evil forces, it is effective to channel that anger to a name they give to a child. Some names are given to confuse the dark forces, as in the following examples:

- Mzondeni (hate him): The parents of this child always felt that when children die as infants, it is because the evil spirits hate them.
- Mbulaleni (kill him): This name was directed at making the evil spirits think that the child is not wanted since the parents pretend that they don't want the child and wouldn't mind if it was killed.
- Mdumazeni (disappoint him): The father of this child had been disappointed repeatedly by losing his children, so he was daring the evil forces to disappoint him again.
- Mlandeni (fetch him): The parents always felt that the children were dying because the evil forces were fetching them and taking them to the unseen world.

- Mcingeni (look for him): The parents of this child consulted a well-known herbalist to protect the pregnant mother from miscarriage and prevent infant mortality, so the name was a dare to the evil spirits to look for the child. The parents were confident that nothing would happen to the child.

Some names are given to show bravery and to scare away the evil forces from the child. These names show strength, courage and determination to fight for the survival of the child. For example:
- Mthinteni (touch him): This name is a dare to the evil spirits to try to take the child away from the parents.
- Mbhasobheni (beware of him): This is a warning to the underworld that they must beware of this child because when he grows up, he is going to be somebody.
- Mlungeleni (be kind to him): This is a plea for the evil spirits to be kind to this child and not cause it any harm.

Some survival names are directed at infants and are used to appeal to the soul of the child not to leave their parents. For example:
- Philasande (survive so we may expand): After his siblings died in infancy, his parents prayed that he would survive, so that the family could grow.
- Khula (grow up): Most of the children in this family died in infancy, so this name appeals to this child to grow up and not die young.

Some names are used to show gratitude for having a child after suffering infant mortality, such as:
- Bongangani (what am I going to offer to show my gratefulness?): The parents of this child were very happy and grateful that it survived.
- Bongathini (what am I going to say in gratitude?): The parents of this child were overwhelmed with gratitude and happiness after the birth of the child.

Some survival names are used to warn sorcerers and witches, to let them know that the parents are aware that they are using *umuthi* to make the family ill. Examples of these kinds of names include:
- Madodanenzani (men, what are you doing?): This name was given to warn the men accused of practising witchcraft to reconsider what they were doing and leave the family alone.
- Mbuzeni (ask him): This name was directed to a family member who was accused of practising witchcraft within the family.
- Skhandamayeza (we are making *umuthi*): This was a warning to a known sorcerer that he must watch out because the people he was bewitching were now using *umuthi* to protect themselves.
- Kwenzakuyashiyana (we are not at the same level): The parents of this child were tired of losing their infant children and consulted a herbalist, who assured them that whoever caused their children's death was going to pay because his *umuthi* was stronger.
- Gwazakwenkunzi (bull's attack): The parents of this child swore that when they found out who caused the death of their children, they would attack him the same way a bull attacks another for territory.

Nicknames are sometimes used instead of personal names in cases where parents have suffered infant mortality. The parents feel that they do not want to give real names to children who will die anyway. They believe that when a child does not have a real name the evil spirits will not take the child. Examples of these kinds of names include Tshovo (soaking wet), Batwana (children), Ntombazane (girl) and Mfana (boy). Not much thought goes into giving nicknames because most of them have no story behind the name. They are sometimes derived from onomatopoeic sounds – for example, Ginsiginsi or Maqinsiqinsi (a chubby baby).

Conclusion

Names discussed in this chapter are pleas for children of parents who have suffered infant mortality to be left alone, often daring the evil spirits to take the child. These names are about the experience of the parents who have suffered infant mortality. The parents personify evil spirits by speaking directly to them and telling them to leave the child alone and give it a chance to live. Obeng (1994) argues that by giving these names, parents are putting on a brave face with regard to their previous losses and are seeking their children's survival and well-being, even though the names themselves, at face value, may seem to imply a lack of worth or respect.

Conclusion

As outlined in the preceding chapters, family members have great respect for the living-dead in Zulu culture and their reverence for the living-dead shapes their behaviour. They rely on the living-dead for protection and provision and thus the maintenance of a healthy relationship between the two parties is crucial. This also extends to individual members of the family. The languages people speak undoubtedly shape their views of the world they live in, as well as the circumstances in which they live. The respect the families in KwaMambulu have for the living-dead is informed by the language they speak.

Anger or rage can be appeased through ritual offerings. The living-dead are entitled to constant communication with their living relatives because Zulu people view life as a continuum and death as a change of state. This is founded on the Zulu belief that life is sacred and permanent.

Lucien Liampawe remarks: 'All the members, therefore, enjoy the same communion and communication with the ancestors, which reinforces the unity and cohesion of the ethnic group' (cited in Akijar 2000: 41). Thus, veneration of the living-dead is closely linked with unity, which is associated with family life. This is because family members venerate the same ancestors. Unity is an African cultural value, which is evident in the Zulu proverb, *Umuntu ngumuntu ngabantu* (a person is because of other people). Maintaining relationships between members of the community is a collective responsibility for every family member. The lives of individuals in African societies are shared. Life would be meaningless if not lived within a community. Community members cannot merely be bystanders or observers in their communities, but must partake in every activity. As John Mbiti makes clear: 'To be human is to belong to the whole community, and to do so involves participating in the beliefs, ceremonies, rituals and festivals of that community' (1969: 3).

Those opposed to polygyny often claim that in such contexts women's emotional instabilities come from being in such 'unstable' situations. But polygyny has a history of acceptance because (for the man) it meant that he would have a large family with many children to carry on his name. There is nothing as important to a Zulu man as having children, especially sons. In polygynous families, sensitive issues stay within the confines of the homestead. In former times, the wife had the right to choose her co-wives to make sure that peace and harmony would prevail within the homestead. It was believed that if the chief wife, in consultation with her subordinates (the second and third wife) chose the fourth one, there would be no fights within the homestead.

However, culture is evolving. Cultural evolution has been perhaps the most dynamic aspect of the lives of African people in the twentieth and twenty-first centuries. Their hopes are raised and set on the future; they work for progress; and they create new myths for the future. It must be noted that even in traditional societies in deep rural areas, culture is not static; and furthermore in areas such as KwaMambulu, it is undergoing change.

'Names are products and reflections of the intimate links between language and socio-cultural organisation' (Herbert 1992: 187). In KwaMambulu, provocative names are still bestowed on children, but most families have embraced the Shembe lifestyle by converting to the Nazareth Baptist Church, which follows the teachings of its founder, Isaiah Shembe. However, this conversion does not require changes in their traditional belief system with regard to the living-dead.

Shifts in culture
Ilobolo
Although the community in KwaMambulu strives to keep things as cultural and traditional as possible, there have been some unavoidable shifts. These come with people who marry into the area and introduce current ways of doing things. For instance, the process of *ilobolo* has been commercialised in our society by both the groom's and the bride's families. Everybody is concerned with what they are going to gain in the end, be it in monetary terms on the part of the bride's family, or in the

form of gifts on the part of the groom's family. Nowadays, most people prefer to spend their money on things that are useful to them as a couple rather than paying *ilobolo* and having *umabo* (giving gifts to the family) at the traditional wedding.

Effects of polygyny

Some people consider polygyny to be only for the uneducated. However, some prominent people who live in urban areas are polygynists. The late Jabu Khanyile, a traditional musician and one of the founding members of the group Bayethe, had two wives who seemed to get along well until his death in 2006. Thereafter, the fight over inheritance started. It turned into a bad family feud, with each wife looking out for her own interests.

In an interview for *Soul* magazine, Oscar nominee Leleti Khumalo (of *Sarafina*, *Yesterday* and *Generations* fame) says her marriage to the theatre tycoon and polygynist Mbongeni Ngema ended because she was not happy. There was always something that made her cry. As a second wife, people assumed that she would get better treatment. However, she says there was no respect. After divorcing his first wife, Ngema wanted to take another wife. Khumalo decided to leave him. She felt strongly about this issue and says: 'The worst part of my marriage was actually polygamy. I have since realized that polygamy is a problem and if I had the opportunity to, I would run a programme to advise young girls and warn them about the dangers of polygamy' (2007: 24). Khumalo believes that the biggest problem about polygamy is jealousy, which becomes inevitable where two or more women are involved. According to Khumalo, men become greedy and only think about themselves and their 'needs'.

The institution of marriage has changed in recent times. Most women, married or otherwise, do not like to share their men, as they feel that this shows that they are not good enough for their husbands. They do not want to be one of many. Much emphasis has been put on the nuclear family. As some women become more educated and empowered, it is clear to them that polygyny is not only risky, but also entails emotional abuse. There has been a great deal of self-discovery for women, as a result of gender and feminist influences.

Religion

Religion has also been affected by ongoing change. African people have realised that they do not need to discard everything African in order to be Christians. There has been a positive change in perception that Africanism should be embraced as it defines who African people are. A significant number of people in KwaMambulu have converted to the Shembe Nazareth Baptist Church because it accepts Africanism. Members of this church wear their traditional attire without fear of being judged and they sing in a traditional way; everything they do is African and that makes them comfortable because they do not have to change to fit in with the demands of Western culture in order to practise the Christian faith.

Dealing with conflict

Confrontation and the airing of discontent is an effective tool for getting people to change their behaviour. Noleen Turner argues:

> Conflict can be constructive. But it can also be destructive. It is this potential for destructive conflict that Zulus seek to minimize in their oral practices. The articulation of the source of conflict may or may not result in actual solutions being arrived at. In some instances the expression in itself may be sufficient to release frustration and pent up emotions (2003: 8).

Modern trends in naming practices

Ihechukwu Madubuike posits: 'A man's name is his most valuable possession. It is his only possession that can survive death. Even the poorest man has a name that can live after death' (1976: 8). African names are bestowed with the hope that the children will follow their names. For example, if parents are grateful that God has given them a child, they might name him Mdumiseni (praise God); if they feel blessed, they might name their child Sibusisiwe (blessed) or Sibusiso (blessing). They might feel lucky to have a child and name that child Nhlanhla (lucky).

Through African names, one comes into contact with family histories and stories that would otherwise not be known. As Adrian Koopman comments:

Zulu names reflect the position of the individual both within the immediate family and the wider family. They show relationships between brothers and sisters, and between parents and children. They reflect the importance of the clan and the importance of the male children in the patrilineal society. They refer to the institution of *ilobolo* as well as to misfortunes such as barrenness and stillbirths. Names may exhort children to appropriate social behaviour. Zulu personal names are without doubt 'social documents' (1989: 45).

Using a person's name in a bad way, such as saying derogatory things about them, can result in being sued for defamation of character in the Western legal context. This shows the importance of a personal name and the significance of treating the name-bearer with dignity and respect. D.B.Z. Ntuli and C.S.Z. Ntuli point out that names now come with monetary value:

> *Kule minyaka edlule igama lomuntu belibiza ishumi lopondo. Kwakuyimali enkulu ishumi lopondo. Yicala elikhulu elalimlahla umuntu qede ahlawuliswe ngeshumi lawopondo. Kwakunjalo ukungcofa igama lomuntu. Nanamuhla kuseyicala elikhulu ukujivaza igama lomuntu ngokuhamba njengehansi utshela abantu ukuthi usobanibani ugile umkhuba omubi. Alisagezwa-ke ngeshumi lawopondo igama elinukubeziwe. Umninilo usekungenela kubammeli, akudle aze adle nenkukhu ethi kwe egcekeni lakho.*
> In the previous years a person's name cost 10 pounds. Ten pounds was a lot of money. It is a serious offence, so the accused was fined ten pounds. That was the price you paid for denigrating a person's name. Even today it still is bad to talk behind a person's back (like a goose) saying so-and-so has done a bad thing. The punishment for denigrating a person's name is no longer ten pounds. The offended person nowadays takes you to his lawyers and sues the hell out of you (1985: 106; my translation).

The advent of missionaries and colonial culture brought many changes to Africa, including to the practices of naming:

To have a new and foreign name ... was a sign of changes from the primitive to the modern world. And the new and foreign name signified this process. This attitude was implanted into people's minds to the extent that even the people (Africans) themselves were not willing to be baptised into the new religions without having new and foreign names accompanied by the act of conversion (Omar, cited in Saarelma-Maunuma 2003: 58).

Themba Moyo points out the difficulties that arose from the differences in naming practices and the clash of cultures as manifested in an individual's name:

Thus we have a pupil obviously given a 'Christian' name by the church, and his father's name was added on as a surname to fit the school requirements. He therefore bore the combined names of 'Patrick Owusu Benefo', only one of which was recognized in his home environment. The others are school or church imposed names, which made him lose his own identity in the bizarre environment of the school and the church. At the western dominated school and church he had one set of names, while in his own cultural and traditional setting, he had a completely different set of names (1996: 13).

Moyo says that at one point 'it was considered old-fashioned and educationally unprogressive to have an African name only' (1996: 13). However, Ntuli and Ntuli complain about the preference of Euro-Western names over African names and argue for the value of African names:

Lafa elihle kakhulu ngokufika kwabelungu nenkolo yobuKristu. Bathi uma siletha amadodakazi ethu esontweni masiwaqambe sithi ngoSibhili, noBhithilizi, noMidilethi, noThilayizina. Yini yona uSibhili? Yini uBhithilizi? Yini uMidilethi? UThilayizina yena yini? Lixabana ngani nenkolo yobuKristu igama lendodakazi yami elithi uShongaziphi? Uma uShongaziphi elanywa uNginikabani kanakalani? UNomkhosi uyinhlamba ngaphi? Ngubani othi izingelosi ziyokwehluleka ukumbiza kahle uthunjana wami zimngenise ekuphileni kwaphakade ngoba ngametha ngathi uBagcinile? Ngamagama aphilayo lana. Ngamagama akhulumayo. Mahle. Ayahlonipheka.

The arrival of the whites with their Christian religion destroyed African culture. When we brought our daughters to church, they said we must give them names like Sybil and Beatrice, Mildred and Tryzina. What is this Sybil? What is Beatrice? What is Mildred? What is Tryzina? What wrong does my daughter's name – Shongaziphi – do to the Christian religion? What is wrong if after Shongaziphi comes Nginikabani? Is the name Nomkhosi an insult? How? Who says that the angels will fail to call my last-born's name and let her into paradise just because I have named her Bagcinile? These names are alive. They have meaning. They are beautiful. They are respectable (1986: 109; my translation).

The Ntulis' resentment of the neglect of African names stems from the fact that by accepting Western religion, African people felt that they had to embrace Western culture as well. More recently, however, many Africans are changing their names and dropping their Euro-Western names. Muntu Xulu says that black people have realised the importance of their names:

Amagama omdabu sekuyiwona asemqoka manje. Singasho ukuthi lokho kwenziwa yikuthi yiwona akhuluma nomuntu nakhuluma ulimi lomdabu kunawesilungu, kumbe athathelwe eMqulwini. Sibona umuntu omnyama esebuyela kokwakhe.

African names are very important nowadays. We can say that it is because they speak to a person in an African language more than the European ones, or those taken from the Bible. We see a black person going back to his roots (1987: 43; my translation).

Much has changed in the naming system. Although some people still use their African names, others have embraced change by giving their children names that are in tune with the times. Koopman notes: 'Names are tending to be less individual and less meaningful . . . It seems today that, especially in the urban areas, certain names have lost their individual quality and have become generalized' (1979: 69).

Minna Saarelma-Maunumaa (2003: 32) asserts that even if personal names do not need to carry information about a culture in order to function as names, they convey a lot of cultural significance. In African cultures, personal names are used for various sociocultural reasons:

> No name is a mere name. There are public and private names, and the names of seniors must often not be used by juniors in addressing them. This is because the name expresses the individual character of a man. It is not a mere handle, but shares in the spiritual reality of man's being . . . In baptisms and the use of Christian names, one finds the difference between a foreign, imposed name, and the one which belongs to the person and his very self. Asked whether such-and-such is his child's Christian name, the father will answer with a direct yes, but asked as to his native name, he will reply with the more profound 'it is he' (Parrinder, cited in Koopman 1986: 15).

Final remarks

When I was conducting field research and interviews, my impression of the community of KwaMambulu was that people are committed to the greater good of the family and the community at large. The community is inclined to keep things traditional, with the men working far off in the cities and the women looking after the homesteads and rearing children.

These people are deeply religious and staunchly believe in the living-dead. They view death as a mere passage into the next life. The living-dead are regarded as part of their daily lives, as omniscient and omnipotent. Rituals are performed to appease the livind-dead. When an event takes place within their homestead that they do not understand, they consult an *isangoma* (diviner), who then speaks to the living-dead on their behalf. They operate within a belief framework that they understand and are committed to. The power the living-dead have over their living descendants is remarkable. Every family member knows and fully understands the role they need to play in harmonising the atmosphere within the homestead. It is these beliefs that force every member of a polygynous family to contain their anger and not fight within the homestead, as that might anger the living-dead.

For many communities on the African continent and particularly in the context of the KwaMambulu community, names are not simply labels. One of the aims of this book is to give insight into Zulu 'traditional' polygynous families and their living conditions. More specifically, it seeks to show how names bestowed on children within polygynous families in respect of the living-dead reflect social behaviour patterns within such situations. In many instances, people in the community of KwaMambulu bestowed names on their children in order to have a voice with regard to any wrongs they believed had been done to them, to communicate their views to the purported wrongdoer, and to seek redress.

At the risk of losing much cultural and traditional inheritance due to the adoption of Western culture, the use of African traditional names should be preserved. I conclude this book with the powerful words of S.M.E. Bhengu.

> For us who are seriously involved in total political liberation of Africa and Africans, the process of total cultural and national reclamation of everything that is African becomes a priority psychologically. As we daily reject those customs, names, mannerisms and norms imposed on us by the Europeans, and thereby used everyday to define our souls, the process of getting our 'righteous' names and the proper definition and recognition of our identity becomes a focus of that struggle. As we daily negate European culture and capitalism as a force that governs our lives, we dialectically re-nourish our appetite for translucent values by taking that which must speak of our identity as a people. Over and over again, the idea of it being impossible for the confused people who are proud of their slave names to get complete independence is reiterated. Through the restructuring of names

and surnames, communal identity will be strengthened, and this will facilitate the reclamation of African identity and culture at all levels (1975: 56).

Appendix

Names in KwaMambulu

Family is big enough
Anele (they are enough – girls)
Aphelele (they are enough in numbers)
Banele (they are enough – them)
Phelelani (it's time you became enough in numbers)
Sanele (we are big enough)
Sphelele (we are enough in numbers)
Sphelelisiwe (we have been made enough)
Zanele (they are enough – girls)

Names beginning with M
Mbangiseni (fight with him over his things)
Mbhasobheni (watch him)
Mbhekeni (watch him)
Mbizwa (the called one)
Mboneni (look at him)
Mbongwa (the thanked one)
Mbukelwa (the one who is always left to do things on his own)
Mbukeni (look at him)
Mbulaleni (kill him)
Mbusiseni (bless him)
Mbuyiselwa (the one who is brought back)
Mbuyiseni (bring him back)
Mbuzeni (ask him)
Mcabangiseni (help him to think)
Mcanukelwa (the one who irritates people)
Mcebiseni (advise him)

Mchazeleni (explain to him)
Mchitheni (destroy him)
Mcingeni (look for him)
Mdindeni (beat him up)
Mdingi (the needy one)
Mdumazeni (embarrass him)
Mfaniseni (who does he look like)
Mfihlelwa (the one they hide things from)
Mfiselwa (the one they wish for)
Mfulathelwa (the one left behind)
Mfungelwa (the one sworn in)
Mgabiselwa (the one they always shows off to)
Mganiseni (arrange a marriage for her)
Mgezeni (wash him/his name)
Mhlabunzima (the world is a difficult place)
Mhlaliseni (stay with him)
Mhlalisi (the bride's keeper)
Mhlekude (he is handsome in far away places)
Mhlekwa (the one they always laugh at)
Mhlengeni (save him)
Mhletshwa (the one they gossip about)
Mhlonipheni (respect him)
Mhlonishwa (the honourable one)
Mkakeni (surround him)
Mkhanyiseni (bring him light)
Mkhanyisi (the one who brings light)
Mkhetheni (choose him)
Mkhethwa (the chosen one)
Mkhohliseni (deceive him)
Mkhombiseni (show him)
Mkhonzeni (like him)
Mkhululeni (free him)
Mkhulunyelwa (the one who is spoken for)
Mlahleni (desert him)
Mlandeni (fetch him)
Mlindwa (the one we have been waiting for)

Mlungeleni (be gentle to him)
Mmiseni (stand by him)
Mnikeni (give him)
Mnikwa (the given one)
Mntukatshelwa (the one who does not listen)
Mnukwa (the one who is accused of witchcraft)
Mphakamiseni (lift him up)
Mphenduleli (the one who speaks on my behalf)
Mphenyi (the detective)
Mphindeni (do that to him again)
Mphiwa (the given one)
Mphumuzeni (free him)
Mqiniseni (make him strong)
Mqondisi (the one who makes things straight)
Mthandeni (like him)
Mthembeni (trust him)
Mthethokayizwani (the rules are conflicting)
Mthinteni (consult with him)
Mthobeleni (submit to him)
Mthokozeleni (be happy for him)
Mtholeni (find him)
Mtholephi (where did you find him)
Mtsheleni (tell him)
Mtshengiseni (show him)
Mtuseni (praise him)
Mvikeleni (protect him)
Mvuseni (wake him up)
Mxoleleni (forgive him)
Myekeni (leave him alone)
Mzameleni (try for him)
Mzamiseni (help him try)
Mzibeni (ignore him)
Mzileni (avoid him)
Mzondeni (hate him)
Mzonzima (the homestead is a difficult place to live in)
Mzumeni (catch him off guard)
Mzungezeni (surround him)

Names derived from a vowel-commencing verb and 'a' (to increase)
Alwande (the family line must increase)
Andile (they have increased)
Asanda (they are still expanding)
Ayanda (they are expanding)
Azande (the girls/boys must increase)
Bandile (they have increased)
Kwanda (the increase)
Luyanda (the family line is expanding)
Mawande (the family must increase)
Philasande (live so that we may increase)
Sandile (we have increased)
Sandiso (the increment)
Sisanda (we are still increasing)
Siyanda (we are increasing)
Usanda (the family is still increasing)
Wandile (the family has expanded)
Zamukwanda (trying to make an increase)
Zandile (the girls have increased in numbers)
Ziyanda (the number of girls / boys has increased)

Names derived from industrialisation
Khalathi (coloured)
Mabhunu (Afrikaans people)
Mshangane (Shangaan/Tsonga person)
Nobelungu (mother of the white people)
Nobesuthu (mother of the Sotho people)
Nomabhomu (mother of bombs)
Nomakula (mother of the Indian people)
Nomangisi (mother of the English-speaking people)
Nomaswazi (mother of the Swazi people)

Names derived from towns
Mdubane (Durban)

Mgababa (Mgababa)
Nomabhayi (mother of Port Elizabeth)
Nomachweba (mother of ports)
Nomagoli (mother of Johannesburg)
Nomakhimbili (mother of Kimberley)

Names ending with -ni (what)
Bafunani (what do they want?)
Bantubazothini (what are people going to say?)
Bashongani (why do they say that?)
Bazothini (what are they going to say?)
Bonani (what did you see?)
Bongangani (what are you thankful about?)
Bongathini (what am I going to use to show I am thankful?)
Bukani (what are you looking at?)
Buyenzeni (what happened when he came back?)
Cabangeni (what did you think about?)
Cebani (what are you planning?)
Celani (what are asking for?)
Dumeleni (what makes you so famous?)
Fikenani (what did you arrive with?)
Fisani (what do you wish for?)
Fisukwenzani (what do you want to do?)
Funani (what do you want?)
Fungeleni (why did you swear?)
Gcinetheni (what did he end up saying?)
Hlaleleni (why are you still here?)
Hlalempini (living in the war zone)
Hlanganani (unite)
Hlebani (what are you gossiping about?)
Hlokomani (celebrate)
Hlulwayini (what is defeating you?)
Hlushwayini (what is troubling you?)
Jaheni (what are you rushing?)
Khalani (what are you crying about?)
Khangwayini (what is attracting you to him/her?)

Khanyisani (give light)
Khawulani (stop)
Kholwangani (what is going to make you believe?)
Khonangani (what causes you to be here?)
Khonani (what is in here?)
Khonjwenzeni (what does he do when he is pointed at?)
Khonzangani (what are you sending your regards with?)
Khonzeni (what do you like so much about him/her?)
Khulumani (speak)
Kwenzakufani (deeds are different)
Kwenzakuni (what kind of doing is this?)
Kwenzeleni (why did you do it?)
Lindeni (what are you waiting for?)
Lungeleni (why are you so kind?)
Melwawubani (who is going to speak on my behalf?)
Mzikayifani (homesteads are different)
Nakowubani (who is going to pay attention to me?)
Ncengani (what are you pleading for?)
Ngenzeleni (what have you done for me?)
Nginikani (what are you giving me?)
Ngizomphani (what am I going to feed her?)
Ngoneni (what have I done wrong?)
Nsukukazifani (days are not the same)
Ntandoni (what kind of a love potion is this?)
Ntombenjani (what kind of a maiden is this?)
Phakamani (lift yourselves up)
Phendulani (answer)
Philangani (what am I going to live with?)
Phiweni (what did you get given?)
Phothani (what are you plaiting?)
Qapheleni (what are you watching?)
Qhoshangani (what are you boasting about?)
Qondeni (what are you intending to do?)
Sabani (what are you scared of?)
Sakhiseni (make us live well)
Senzeni (what have we done wrong?)

Setheni (what has he/she said?)
Shongani (why do you say that?)
Sibangani (what are we fighting about?)
Simethembeni (what do we trust about him?)
Sizwayini (what is going to help you?)
Solani (what are you suspecting?)
Songeleni (why did you swear?)
Sweleni (what do you need?)
Thandonjani (why do you like that particular life?)
Thangithini (what do you want me to say?)
Thembeni (what are you trusting?)
Thuleleni (why are you so quiet?)
Tshelwawubani (who told you?)
Vumeleni (why did agree to this?)
Zamukwenzani (what are you trying to do?)
Zibelani (why are you ignoring me?)
Zodlani (what am I or are we going to eat?)
Zokwenzani (what am I going to do?)
Zotholani (what are you going to gain?)
Zuzani (what are you going to gain?)
Zwabethini (what do you hear them say?)
Zweni (what did you hear?)

Names ending with -phi? (where or which)
Bhekamuphi (which one should we watch?)
Bhekephi (in which direction are you looking?)
Bizwephi (who invited you?)
Bulewephi (where are you bewitched?)
Buselaphi (where are you going to rule?)
Buyelaphi (where is she coming back to?)
Buzaliphi (which one are you asking about?)
Fihlwaphi (where are we going to hide her?)
Fikelephi (where did she arrive at?)
Hambephi (where did you go?)
Hlalephi (where did you sit?)
Hleziphi (where are we staying?)

Khokhaziphi (which one are you paying?)
Khongaphi (where are you starting *ilobolo* negotiations?)
Khonzaphi (where are you passing your regards?)
Khulelaphi (where are you growing up?)
Ntombizaphi (where are these girls from?)
Nyathelephi (where did you put your foot?)
Phephelaphi (where are we going to be safe?)
Phethelaphi (where are you going to end up?)
Qhamukephi (where did she come from?)
Sakhamuphi (which one are you building?)
Sakhephi (where are we living?)
Shiyaliphi (which one are you leaving out?)
Sholiphi (which one are you referring to?)
Shongaziphi (which ones are you talking about?)
Sibangaliphi (which one are we fighting over?)
Singaphi (on which side are we?)
Thandephi (where is your future mother-in-law's house?)
Thokozaphi (where are you having fun?)
Tshenwephi (where did you get your information from?)
Velephi (where did you come from?)
Vimbephi (where am I stopping you?)
Zithathephi (where did you get that from?)
Zobephi (where will you be?)
Zothephi (you don't think she is humble, do you?)

Names with the possessive -akhe (his)
Bhekokwakhe (he is watching his)
Busangokwakhe (he is a king of his own castle)
Falakhe (his inheritance)
Fihlokwakhe (he is hiding his)
Fundakwezakhe (he has realised things on his own)
Funokwakhe (he wants his)
Gcinokwakhe (he is keeping his)
Gqibokwakhe (he is hiding his things)
Hlomesakhe (he is protecting himself with his shield)
Khethowakhe (he is choosing his own)

Khohlwayezakhe (he/she has forgotten his own affairs)
Kwazikwakhe (his own knowledge)
Kwenzakwakhe (his own doing)
Phathokwakhe (he is handling his)
Phumowakhe (he is building his own homestead)
Qondokwakhe (he understands his)
Sebenzeyakhe (he is working his own money)
Shokwakhe (he is saying his)
Simosakhe (his circumstance)
Sonosakhe (his sin)
Thandowakhe (he loves his)
Thathezakhe (he is taking his)
Thathokwakhe (he is taking his own)
Thembokwakhe (he trusts his)
Zamokwakhe (he is trying his own)
Zibokwakhe (he is ignoring his)

Names with *umuzi* (home) as a stem
Mzikabani (whose home is this?)
Mzikawubongwa (the home that has not been thanked)
Mzikawukhalelwa (the home is not something you can cry over)
Mzikayifani (homesteads are different)
Mzikayise (his father's house)
Mziweqili (a home of a trickster)
Mzobanzi (huge home)
Mzokhanyayo (a home that is full of light)
Mzokhethiwe (the chosen home)
Mzokhona (the family is here)
Mzokhulayo (the expanding family)
Mzomuhle (a nice home)
Mzonjani (what kind of a home is this?)
Mzonzima (a dangerous home)
Mzothulayo (a quiet home)
Mzovukayo (the family has been revived)
Mzuvele (the family has appeared)
Mzwakhe (his home)

Mzwamandla (a house of power)
Mzwandile (the family has expanded)
Mzwempi (a home of war)
Mzwendoda (a man's homestead)
Mzwenduna (a headman's homestead)
Mzwenhlanhla (a home of luck)
Mzwenkosi (the house of the Lord)
Mzwethu (our home)
Mzwoxolo (a home of peace)

Select Bibliography

Agadjanian, V. and A.C. Ezeh. 2000. 'Polygyny, Gender Relations, and Reproduction in Ghana'. *Journal of Comparative Family Studies* 31 (4): 427–41.

Agar, Michael. 1980. *The Professional Stranger: An Informal Introduction to Ethnography*. New York: Academic Press.

Agbontaen-Eghafona, Kokunre. 2007. 'Factors in Personal Naming and Name Change in Post-Colonial Southern Nigeria'. *Nomina Africana* 21 (1–2): 105–25.

Agnew, Neil and Sandra Pyke. 1982. *The Science Game: The Introduction to Research in Behavioural Sciences*. 3rd ed. Englewood Cliffs, NJ: Prentice-Hall.

Agyekum, Kofi. 2006. 'The Sociolinguistic of Akan Personal Names'. *Nordic Journal of African Studies* 15 (2): 206–35.

Akijar, Livingstone. 2000. 'Is the Interpretation of Christ as the "Ancestor of the Church" Compatible with the Christian Doctrine? A Study of Christology and Ecclesiology of Charles Nyamiti'. Master's thesis, University of Natal, Pietermaritzburg.

Alford, Richard. 1988. *Naming and Identity: A Cross-Cultural Study of Personal Naming Practices*. New Haven: HRAF Press.

Al-Krenawi, Alean. 1999. 'The Story of Bedouin-Arab Women in a Polygamous Marriage'. *Women's Studies International Forum* 22 (5): 497–509.

Amanze, James. 2003. 'Christianity and Ancestor Veneration in Botswana'. *Studies in World Christianity* 9 (1): 43–59.

Anderson, Allan. 1991. *Moya: The Holy Spirit in an African Context*. Pretoria: Unisa Press.

Bae, Choon Sup. 2007. 'Ancestor Worship and the Challenges it Poses to the Christian Mission and Ministry'. PhD diss., University of South Africa, Pretoria.

Bass, Bernard M. 1990. *Bass and Stogdill's Handbook of Leadership: Theory, Research, and Managerial Applications*. New York: The Free Press.

Bate, Stuart. 1995. *Inculturation and Healing: Coping-Healing in South African Christianity*. Pietermaritzburg: Cluster Publications.

Beasley, Christine. 2008. 'Rethinking Hegemonic Masculinity in a Globalizing World'. *Men and Masculinities* 11 (1): 86–103.

Beattie, John H. 1957. 'Nyoro Personal Names'. *Uganda Journal* 21: 99–106.

Berglund, Axel-Ivar. 1976. *Zulu Thought-Patterns and Symbolism*. London: C. Hurst & Co.

Bhengu, S.M.E. 1975. *Chasing Gods Not Our Own*. Pietermaritzburg: Shuter & Shooter.

Blackbeard, David and Graham Lindegger. 2007. ' "Building a Wall around Themselves": Exploring Adolescent Masculinity and Abjection with Photo-Biographical Research'. *South African Journal of Psychology* 37 (1): 25–46.

Bockie, Simon. 1993. *Death and the Invisible Powers: The World of Kongo Belief*. Bloomington: Indiana University Press.

Bongmba, Elias K. 2007. 'Witchcraft and the Christian Church: Ethical Implications'. In *Imagining Evil: Witchcraft Beliefs and Accusations in Contemporary Africa*, edited by Gerrie ter Haar, 113–42. Trenton, NJ: Africa World Press.

Boserup, Ester. 1970. *Women's Role in Economic Development*. London: George Allen and Unwin.

———. 1985. 'Population, the Status of Women and Rural Development'. *Population and Development Review* 15: 45–60.

Brennen, Tim. 2000. 'On the Meaning of Personal Names: A View from Cognitive Psychology'. *Names* 48 (2): 139–46.

Brinkmann, Svend and Steinar Kvale. 2009. *Interviews: Learning the Craft of Qualitative Research Interviewing*. Thousand Oaks, CA: Sage.

Brod, Harry, ed. 1987. *The Making of Masculinities: The New Men's Studies*. Boston: Allen & Unwin.

Brown, Gillian and George Yule. 1983. *Discourse Analysis*. Cambridge: Cambridge University Press.

Brown, Judith E. 1981. 'Polygyny and Family Planning in Sub-Saharan Africa'. *Studies in Family Planning* 12 (8/9): 322–6.

Caldwell, J.C., P.H. Reddy and Pat Caldwell. 1983. 'The Cause of Marriage Change in South India'. *Populations Studies* 37 (3): 343–61.

Chodorow, Nancy. 1995. 'Gender as a Personal and Cultural Construction'. *Signs* 20 (3): 516–44.

Chuks-Orji, Ogonna. 1972. *Names from Africa*. Chicago: Johnson.

Connell, R.W. 1987. *Gender and Power: Society, the Person, and Sexual Politics*. Cambridge: Polity Press.

Connell, R.W. 1995. *Masculinities*. Cambridge: Polity Press.

Connell, R.W. and James Messerschmidt. 2005. 'Hegemonic Masculinity: Rethinking the Concept'. *Gender & Society* 19 (6): 829–59.

Cook, Rebecca J. and Lisa M. Kelly. 2006. *Polygyny and Canada's Obligations under International Human Rights Law*. Ottawa: Department of Justice of Canada.

Cowan, Jane, Marie-Bénédicte Dembour and Richard Wilson, eds. 2001. *Culture and Rights: Anthropological Perspectives*. Cambridge: Cambridge University Press.

Creswell, John W. 2009 *Research Design: Qualitative, Quantitative and Mixed Methods Approaches*. 3rd ed. Thousand Oaks, CA: Sage.

Crosby, K.H. 1937. 'Polygamy in Mende Country'. *Africa* 10 (3): 249–64.

Dangor, Suleman. 2001. 'Historical Perspective, Current Literature and an Opinion Survey among Muslim Women in Contemporary South Africa: A Case Study'. *Journal of Muslim Minority Affairs* 21 (1): 109–29.

Davies, Nick and Gill Eagle. 2013. 'Conceptualising the Paternal Function: Maleness, Masculinity, or Thirdness?' *Contemporary Psychoanalysis* 49 (4): 559–85.

Delius, Peter and Clive Glaser. 2004. 'The Myths of Polygamy: A History of Extra-Marital and Multi-Partnership Sex in South Africa'. *South African Historical Journal* 50 (1): 84–114.

Diamond, Michael J. 2006. 'Masculinity Unraveled: The Roots of Male Identity and the Shifting Male Ego Ideals throughout Life'. *Journal of the American Psychoanalytic Association* 5 (4): 1099–130.

Dorian, Nancy C. 1970. 'A Substitute Name System in the Scottish Highlands'. *American Anthropologist* 72 (2): 303–19.

Doucet, Andrea. 2015. 'Parental Responsibilities: Dilemmas of Measurement and Gender Equality'. *Journal of Marriage and Family* 77 (1): 224–42.

Dovlo, Elom. 2007. 'Witchcraft in Contemporary Ghana'. In *Imagining Evil: Witchcraft Beliefs and Accusations in Contemporary Africa*, edited by Gerrie ter Haar, 67–92. Trenton, NJ: Africa World Press.

Downs. James F. 1971. *Cultures in Crisis*. Beverly Hills: Glencoe Press.

Duncan, Greg J. and Jeanne Brooks-Gunn, eds. 1997. *Consequences of Growing Up Poor*. New York: Russell Sage Foundation.

Dundes, Alan. 1983. 'Defining Identity through Folklore'. In *Identity: Personal and Sociocultural*, edited by Anita Jacobson-Widding, 235–61. Uppsala: Almquist and Wissel.

Dwane, S. 1975. 'Polygamy'. In *Church and Marriage in Modern Africa*, edited by T.D. Verryn, 221–37. Pretoria: Ecumenical Research Unit.

Dziva, Douglas. 1997. 'A Critical Examination of Patterns of Research in the Academic Study of Shona Traditional Religion, with Special Reference to Methodological Consideration'. PhD diss., University of Natal, Pietermaritzburg.

Earth, Barbara and Sabitri Sthapit. 2002. 'Uterine Prolapse in Rural Nepal: Gender and Human Rights Implications. A Mandate for Development'. *Culture, Health and Sexuality* 4 (3): 281–96.

Eiselen, Werner and Isaac Schapera. 1950. 'Kinship and Marriage among the Tswana'. In *African Systems of Kinship and Marriage*, edited by Alfred Radcliffe-Brown and Daryll Forde, 140–65. Oxford: Oxford University Press.

Elá, Jean-Marc. 1995. *My Faith as an African*. Maryknoll, NY: Orbis Books.

Elbedour, Salman, Anthony J. Onwuegbuzie, Corin Caridine and Hasan Abu-Saad. 2002. 'The Effect of Polygamous Marital Structure on Behavioral, Emotional, and Academic Adjustment in Children: A Comprehensive Review of the Literature'. *Clinical Child and Family Psychology Review* 5 (4): 255–71.

Ezeh, Alex C. 1997. 'Polygyny and Reproductive Behaviour in Sub-Saharan Africa: A Contextual Analysis'. *Demography* 34 (3): 355–68.
Fanon, Frantz. 2004. *The Wretched of the Earth*. New York: Grove Press.
Finnegan, Ruth. 1970. *Oral Literature in Africa*. Oxford: Oxford University Press.
Franks, David D. and Joseph Marolla. 1976. 'Efficacious Action and Social Approval as Interacting Dimensions of Self-Esteem: A Tentative Formulation through Construct Validation'. *Sociometry* 39 (4): 324–41.
Franzosi, Roberto. 1998. 'Narrative Analysis – Or Why (and How) Sociologists Should be Interested in Narrative'. *Annual Review of Sociology* 24: 517–54.
Gamble, R. 1996. 'Black South African Given Names, Stereotyping and First Grade Academic Achievement'. Honours thesis, University of Ulster, Coleraine.
Gardiner, Alan. 1957. *The Theory of Proper Names: A Controversial Essay*. Oxford: Oxford University Press.
Garenne, Michel and Etienne van de Walle. 1989. 'Polygyny and Fertility among the Seerer of Senegal'. *Population Studies* 43 (2): 267–83.
Gelfand, Donna M. 1968. *African Crucible: An Ethico-Religious Study with Special Reference to the Shona-Speaking People*. Cape Town: Juta.
Goodrich, Thelma Jean, Cheryl Rampage, Barbara Ellman and Kris Halstead. 1988. *Feminist Family Therapy: A Casebook*. New York: W.W. Norton.
Gould, Eric D., Omer Moav and Avi Simhon. 2008. 'The Mystery of Monogamy'. *The American Economic Review* 98 (1): 333–57.
Grant, Michael. 2006. *Saint Peter*. London: Weidenfeld & Nicolson.
Gray, James J. and Rebecca L. Ginsberg. 2007. 'Muscle Dissatisfaction: An Overview of Psychological and Cultural Research and Theory'. In *The Muscular Ideal: Psychological, Social and Medical Perspectives*, edited by J. Kevin Thompson and Guy Cafri, 15–40. Washington, DC: American Psychological Association.
Gray, Joseph P. 1998. 'Ethnographic Atlas Codebook'. *World Cultures* 10 (1): 86–136.
Grossbard, Shoshana Amyra. 1993. *On the Economics of Marriage: A Theory of Marriage, Labor and Divorce*. Boulder, CO: Westview.
Hallen, Barry and J. Olubi Sodipo. 1986. *Knowledge, Belief and Witchcraft: Analytic Experiments in African Philosophy*. Stanford: Stanford University Press.
Hammersley, Martyn and Paul Atkinson. 1983. *Ethnography: Principles in Practice*. London: Routledge.
Hammond-Tooke, W.D., ed. 1974. *The Bantu-Speaking Peoples of Southern Africa*. London: Routledge.
Harries, Jim. 2010. 'Witchcraft, Culture, and Theology in African Development'. *African Nebula* 2: 138–52.
Harris, Marvin. 1988. *Culture, People, Nature: An Introduction to General Anthropology*. 5th ed. New York: Harper & Row.
Hayase, Yasuko and Kao-Lee Liaw. 1997. 'Factors on Polygamy in Sub-Saharan Africa: Findings Based on the Demographic and Health Surveys'. *The Developing Economies* 35 (3): 293–327.

Helander, Gunnar. 1958. *Must We Introduce Monogamy? A Study of Polygamy as a Mission Problem in South Africa*. Pietermaritzburg: Shuter & Shooter.

Herbert, Robert K., ed. 1992. *Language and Society in Africa: The Theory and Practice of Sociolinguistics*. Johannesburg: Witwatersrand University Press.

Herbert, Robert K. and Senni Bogatsu. 2001. *Changes in Northern Sotho and Tswana Personal Naming Patterns*. Berkeley: University of California Press.

Hinkin, Timothy R. and Chester A. Schriesheim. 1989. 'Development and Application of New Scales to Measure the French and Raven (1959) Bases of Social Power'. *Journal of Applied Psychology* 74 (4): 561–7.

Hlophe, D. and B. Ngcaweni. 2010. 'The Joys of Polygamy for Middle-Class Women'. *Sunday Times*, 24 January.

Hoelter, Jon W. 1985. 'A Structural Theory of Personal Consistency'. *Social Psychology Quarterly* 48 (2): 118–29.

Idowu, E. Bọlaji. 1973. *African Traditional Religion: A Definition*. New York: Orbis Press.

Jacoby, Hanan G. 1995. 'The Economics of Polygyny in Sub-Saharan Africa: Female Productivity and the Demand for Wives in Côte d'Ivoire'. *Journal of Political Economy* 103 (5): 938–71.

Jebadu, Alexander. 2006. *African Ancestral Veneration and the Possibility of its Incorporation into the Catholic Devotion*. Rome: Editrice Pontifica Universita Gregoriana.

Jonas, Obonye. 2012. 'The Practice of Polygamy under the Scheme of the Protocol to the African Charter on Human and People's Rights on the Rights of Women in Africa: A Critical Appraisal'. *Journal of African Studies and Development* 4 (5): 142–9.

Joseph, John E. 2004. *Language and Identity*. London: Macmillan.

Jousse, Hélène. 2004. 'A New Contribution to the History of Pastoralism in West Africa'. *Journal of African Archaeology* 2 (2): 187–201.

Junod, Henri Alexandre. 1927. *The Life of a South African Tribe*. London: Macmillan.

Kanyoro, Musimbi. 2002. *Introducing Feminist Cultural Hermeneutics: An African Perspective*. Sheffield: Sheffield Academic Press.

Kazianga, Harounan and Stefan Klonner. 2009. 'The Intra-household Economics of Polygyny: Fertility and Child Mortality in Rural Mali'. Economics Working Paper Series 0902, Oklahoma State University, Department of Economics and Legal Studies in Business.

Kgatla, Selaelo Thias. 2007. 'Containment of Witchcraft Accusations in South Africa: A Search for a Transformational Approach to Curb the Problem'. In *Imagining Evil: Witchcraft Beliefs and Accusations in Contemporary Africa*, edited by Gerrie ter Haar, 269–92. Trenton, NJ: Africa World Press.

Khathide, Goodman Agrippa. 2003. 'Spirit in the First-Century Jewish World, Luke-Acts and in the African Context: An Analysis'. PhD diss., University of South Africa, Pretoria.

Khoabane, Pinky. 2010. 'Women Are Ready to Play Polygamists at Their Own Game'. *Sunday Times*, 8 August.

Khumalo, Leleti. 2007. 'I Survived a Polygamous Marriage'. *Soul* (March): 24.

Kidwai, Mushir Hosain. n.d. *Polygamy*. London: The Central Islamic Society.

Kisembo, Benezeri, Laurenti Magesa and Aylward Shorter. 1977. *African Christian Marriage*. South Hampton: Camelot.

Koopman, Adrian. 1979. 'Male and Female Names in Zulu'. *African Studies* 38 (1): 67–80.

———. 1986. 'The Social and Literary Aspects of Zulu Personal Names'. Master's thesis, University of Natal, Pietermaritzburg.

———. 1989. 'The Aetiology of Zulu Personal Names'. *Nomina Africana* 3 (2): 31–46.

———. 2002. *Zulu Names*. Pietermaritzburg: University of Natal Press.

Krige, Eileen Jensen. 1950. *The Social Systems of the Zulus*. Pietermaritzburg: Shuter & Shooter.

Krige, Eileen Jensen and John L. Comaroff, eds. 1981. *Essays on African Marriage in Southern Africa*. Cape Town: Juta.

Kubheka, I.S. 1988. *Ulaka lwabaNguni*. Pietermaritzburg: Reach Publishers.

Kuria, Gibson Kamau. 1987. 'The African or Customary Marriage in Kenyan Law'. In *Transformations of African Marriage*, edited by David Parkin and David Nyamwaya, 283–306. Manchester: Manchester University Press.

Kuschel, Rolf. 1988. *Vengeance is the Reply: Blood Feuds and Homicides on Bellona Island*. Copenhagen: Dansk Psykologisk Forlag.

Lambert, Michael. 2000. 'Classical Athenian and Traditional African Ethics: The Hermeneutics of Shame and Guilt'. *South African Journal for Folklore Studies* 11 (1): 41–55.

Landar, Herbert. 1966. *Language and Culture*. New York: Oxford University Press.

Langacker, Ronald. 1994. 'The Limits of Continuity: Discreteness in Cognitive Semantics'. In *Continuity in Linguistic Semantics*, edited by Catherine Fuchs and Bernard Victorri, 9–20. New York: Harper & Row.

Lewis, I.M. 1976. *Social Anthropology in Perspective: The Relevance of Social Anthropology*. Cambridge: Cambridge University Press.

Lewis, J. Johnson. 2020. 'What is the Practice of Polyandry: Marriage Customs in the Tibetan Himalayan Highlands'. *ThoughtCo.*, 6 February. https://www.thoughtco.com/polyandry-in-tibet-3528444.

Linnekin, Jocelyn S. 1983. 'Defining Tradition: Variations on the Hawaiian Identity'. *American Ethnologist* 10 (2): 241–52.

Lombard, Carol. 2008. 'An Ethnolinguistic Study of Niitsitapi Personal Names'. Master's thesis, University of South Africa, Pretoria.

Louwrens, L.J. 1993. 'Semantic Change in Loan Words'. *South African Journal of African Languages* 13 (1): 8–16.

Lui, Lake. 2013. *Re-negotiating Gender: Household Division of Labor When She Earns More Than He Does*. Dordrecht: Springer.
Mac an Ghaill, Máirtín. 1994. *The Making of Men: Masculinities, Sexualities and Schooling*. Buckingham: Open University Press.
Machaba, Mbali. 2005. 'Naming, Identity and the Renaissance, in a South African Context'. PhD diss., University of KwaZulu-Natal, Pietermaritzburg.
Madhavan, Sangeetha. 2002. 'Best of Friends and Worst of Enemies: Competition and Collaboration in Polygyny'. *Ethnology* 41 (1): 69–84.
Madubuike, Ihechukwu. 1976. *A Handbook of African Names*. Colorado Springs: Three Continents Press.
Magesa, Laurenti. 1997. *African Religion: The Moral Traditions of Abundant Life*. Maryknoll, NY: Orbis Books.
Maillu, David. 1988 *Our Kind of Polygamy*. Nairobi: Heinemann Kenya.
Makondo, Livingstone. 2009. 'An Investigation into Anthroponyms of the Shona Society'. PhD diss., University of South Africa, Pretoria.
Mammen, Kristin. 2009. *All for One or Each for Her Own: Do Polygamous Families Share and Share Alike?* Columbia: Columbia University Press.
Mapanje, Jack and Landeg White, eds. 1983. *Oral Poetry from Africa*. London: Longman.
Markus, Hazel Rose and Shinobu Kitayama. 1994. 'Culture and the Self: How Cultures Influence the Way We View Ourselves'. In *People: Psychology from a Cultural Perspective*, edited by David Matsumoto, 17–37. San Francisco: Brooks/Cole.
Marshall, Catherine and Gretchen Rossman. 2011. *Designing Qualitative Research*. 5th ed. Thousand Oaks, CA: Sage.
Mathangwane, Joyce and Sheena Gardner. 1998. 'Language Attitudes as Portrayed by the Use of English and African Names in Botswana'. *Nomina Africana* 12 (2): 74–87.
Mbeki, Thabo. 'Statement on Behalf of the ANC on the Occasion of the Adoption by the Constitutional Assembly of "The Republic of South Africa Constitution Bill 1996", Cape Town, 1996/05/08' ('I am an African' Speech). http://www.mbeki.org/2016/06/06/statement-on-behalf-of-the-anc-on-the-occasion-of-the-adoption-by-the-constitutional-assembly-of-the-republic-of-south-africa-constitution-bill-1996-cape-town-19960508/.
Mbiti, John S. 1969. *African Religions and Philosophy*. 2nd ed. Oxford: Heinemann Educational Publishers.
———. 1970. *Concepts of God in Africa*. London: Society for Promoting Christian Knowledge.
Miller, Nathan. 1927. 'Some Aspects of the Name in Culture-History'. *American Journal of Sociology* 32 (4): 585–600.
Mkhize, Zamambo Valentine. 2011. 'Polygyny and Gender: Narratives of Professional Zulu Women in Peri-urban Areas of Contemporary KwaZulu-Natal'. Master's thesis, University of KwaZulu-Natal, Durban.

———. 2015. 'Polygyny and Gender: The Gendered Narratives of Adults Who Were Raised in Polygynous Families'. PhD diss., University of KwaZulu-Natal, Durban.
Mönnig, H.O. 1967. *The Pedi*. Pretoria: J.L. van Schaik.
Morrell, Robert. 1994. 'Masculinity and the White Boys' Boarding Schools of Natal, 1880–1930'. *Perspectives in Education* 15 (4): 27–52.
———. 1998. 'Of Boys and Men: Masculinity and Gender in Southern African Studies'. *Journal of Southern African Studies* 24: 605–30.
———, ed. 2001. *Changing Men in Southern Africa*. Pietermaritzburg: University of Natal Press.
Morrell, Robert, Rachel Jewkes and Graham Lindegger. 2012. 'Hegemonic Masculinity/Masculinities in South Africa: Culture, Power, and Gender Politics'. *Men and Masculinities* 15 (1): 11–30.
Mouton, Johann and H.C. Marais. 1988. *Basic Concepts in the Methodology of the Social Sciences*. Pretoria: HSRC Press.
Moyo, Themba. 1996. 'Personal Names and Naming Practices in Northern Malawi'. *Nomina Africana* 10 (1&2): 10–19.
Msimang, C.T. 1975. *Buzani kuMkabayi*. Pretoria: De Jager Haum Publishers.
———. 1991. *Kusadliwa ngoludala*. 2nd ed. Pietermaritzburg: Shuter & Shooter.
Mutembei, A.K. and J.L.P. Lugalla. 2002. 'Using Narratives to Understand People's Experience on AIDS: Examples from Oral Poetry of the Bahaya of Bukoba, Tanzania'. Unpublished paper delivered at the Conference on Language and Literature and the Discourse on HIV/AIDS in Africa, hosted at the University of Botswana, Gaborone, June.
Mutran, Elizabeth and Peter J. Burke. 1979. 'Feeling "Useless": A Common Component of Young and Old Adult Identities'. *Research on Aging* 1: 188–212.
Nasimiyu-Wasike, Anne. 1992. 'Christianity and the African Rituals of Birth and Naming'. In *The Will to Arise: Women, Tradition, and the Church in Africa*, edited by Mercy Amba Oduyoye and Rachel Angogo Kanyoro, 40–53. New York: Orbis Books.
Nasimiyu-Wasike, Anne and Jesse N.K. Mugambi, eds. 1992. *Moral and Ethical Issues in African Christianity: Exploratory Essays in Moral Theology*. Nairobi: Initiatives Publishers.
Neethling, S.J. 1995. 'Names and Naming in Xhosa'. *Name Studies* 1: 956–9.
Nencel, L. 2007. 'Anthropology'. In *Introduction to Gender: Social Science Perspective*, edited by Jennifer Marchbank and Gayle Letherby, 89–109. London: Pearson Education.
Ngondo a Pitshandenge, Iman. 1994. 'Marriage Law in Sub-Saharan Africa'. In *Nuptiality in Sub-Saharan Africa: Contemporary Anthropological and Demographic Perspectives*, edited by Caroline Bledsoe and Gilles Pison, 117–29. Oxford: Clarendon Press.

Ngubane, Sihawukele Emmanuel. 2000. 'Reclaiming Our Names: Shifts Post-1994 in Zulu Naming Practices'. PhD diss., University of Natal, Durban.

Nicolaisen, W.F.H. 1976. 'Words as Names'. *Onoma* 20 (1): 142–63.

Ntuli, D.B.Z. and C.S.Z. Ntuli. 1985. *Amawisa*. Pietermaritzburg: Shuter & Shooter.

———. 1986. *Izizenze*. Pietermaritzburg: Shuter & Shooter.

Nurohmah, Leli. 2003. 'Poligami: Saatnya Melihat Realitas'. *Jurnal Perempuan* 31: 31–45.

Nyabwari, Bernard Gechiko and Dickson Nkonge Kagema. 2014. 'The Impact of Magic and Witchcraft in the Social, Economic, Political and Spiritual Life of African Communities'. *International Journal of Humanities, Social Sciences and Education* 1 (5): 9–18.

Nyamiti, Charles. 1984. *Christ as Our Ancestor: Christology from an African Perspective*. Gweru: Mambo Press.

Nyirongo, Lenard. 1997. *The Gods of Africa or the God of the Bible? The Snares of African Traditional Religion in Biblical Perspective*. Potchefstroom: IPS.

Obeng, Samuel Gyasi. 1994. 'Language and Politics: Indirectness in Political Discourse'. *Discourse and Society* 8 (1): 49–83.

———. 2001. *African Anthroponymy: An Ethnopragmatic and Morphonological Study of Personal Names in Akan and Some African Societies*. München: Lincom Europa.

Oliello, John Komo. 2005. 'The Gospel and African Culture: Polygamy as a Challenge to the Anglican Church of Tanzania – Diocese of Mara'. Master's thesis, University of KwaZulu-Natal, Pietermaritzburg.

Olupona, Jacob K. 2000. *African Spirituality: Forms, Meanings and Expressions*. New York: Crossroad Publishing.

O'Neill, Tam and Pilar Domingo. 2015. 'The Power to Decide: Women, Decision-Making and Gender Equality'. Overseas Development Institute Briefing Paper. https://odi.org/en/publications/the-power-to-decide-women-decision-making-and-gender-equality/.

Ong, Walter. 1977. *Interfaces of the Word*. Ithaca: Cornell University Press.

Onukawa, M.C. 1998. 'Anthropolinguistic Study of Igbo Market-Day Nicknames'. *Journal of African Cultural Studies* 11 (1): 73–83.

Oppong, Christine. 1974. *Marriage among a Matrilineal Elite: A Family Study of Ghanaian Senior Civil Servants*. Cambridge: Cambridge University Press.

Orobator, Agbonkhianmeghe E. 2008. *Theology Brewed in an African Pot: An Introduction to Christian Doctrine from an African Perspective*. Nairobi: Pauline Publications.

Oyefeso, Adenekan O. and Ademola R. Adegoke. 1992. 'Psychological Adjustment of Yoruba Adolescents as Influenced by Family Type: A Research Note'. *Journal of Child Psychology and Psychiatry* 33 (4): 785–8.

Oyewumi, Oyeronke. 1997. *The Invention of Women: Making an African Sense of Western Gender Discourses*. Minneapolis: University of Minnesota Press.

Ozkan, Mustafa, Abdurrahman Altindag, Remzi Oto and Esin Sentunali. 2006. 'Mental Health Aspects of Turkish Women from Polygamous versus Monogamous Families'. *International Journal of Social Psychiatry* 52 (3): 214–20.
Palmer, Frank Robert. 1981. *Semantics*. New York: Cambridge University Press.
Parrinder, Geoffrey. 1954. *African Traditional Religion*. London: Hutchinson's University Library.
———. 1958. *The Bible and Polygamy: A Study of Hebrew and Christian Teaching*. London: Society for Promoting Christian Knowledge.
Pfukwa, Charles. 2007. 'The Function and Significance of War Names in the Zimbabwean Armed Conflict (1966–1979)'. DLitt diss., University of South Africa, Pretoria.
Pfukwa, Charles and Lawrie Barnes. 2008. 'The Animal in Guerrilla War Names in the Zimbabwean War of Liberation'. *Nomina Africana* 22 (1&2): 77–103.
Phiri, G. and F. Tembo. 2004. *Women of Mirrors*. Lusaka: Kabulong Press.
Poelma, Renske Thalia and Rosan Stuijt. 2015. 'Gender, Sexuality and HIV/AIDS Entwined: A Gender Sensitive Approach to HIV/AIDS Stigma, Discourse and Behaviour in Ramaswikana, Limpopo, South Africa'. Bachelor of Cultural Anthropology and Developmental Sociology. Utrecht: Utrecht University. https://dspace.library.uu.nl/bitstream/handle/1874/315997/Poelma%2C%20Renske%20Thalia%20en%20Stuijt%2C%20Rosan.pdf?sequence=2&isAllowed=y.
Pyke, Karen D. and Denise L. Johnson. 2003. 'Asian American Women and Racialized Femininities: "Doing" Gender across Cultural Worlds'. *Gender and Society* 17 (1): 33–53.
Raper, Peter. 1986. 'Research Possibilities in Onomastics'. In *Names 1983: Proceedings of the Second Southern African Names Congress, Pretoria, 13–15 September 1983*, 65–8. Pretoria: Human Sciences Research Council.
———. 1987. 'Aspects of Onomastic Theory'. *Nomina Africana* 1 (2): 78–91.
Ro, Y.C. 1988. *Ancestor Worship: From the Perspective of Korean Traditions*. Grand Rapids, MI: Eerdmans.
Roberts, Simon A. 1979. *Order and Dispute: An Introduction to Legal Anthropology*. New York: Penguin.
Ross, Susan Deller. 2002. 'Polygyny as a Violation of Women's Right to Equality in Marriage: An Historical, Comparative and International Human Rights Overview'. *Delhi Law Review* 24: 22–34.
Russo, Sandra L. and Suzanna D. Smith. 2006. 'Women in the Two-Thirds World'. In *Families in Global and Multicultural Perspective*, edited by Bron B. Ingoldsby and Suzanna D. Smith. Thousand Oaks, CA: Sage.
Saarelma-Maunumaa, Minna. 2003. *Edhina Ekogidho: Names as Links – The Encounter between African and European Anthroponymic Systems among the Ambo People in Namibia*. Helsinki: Finnish Literature Society.
Sanders, Peter. 1975. *Moshoeshoe, Chief of the Sotho*. London: Heinemann.

Sarpong, Peter. 1974. *Ghana in Retrospect: Some Aspects of Ghanaian Culture*. Accra: Ghana Publishing Corporation.
Schaefer, Richard T. and Robert P. Lamm. 1992. *Sociology*. 4th ed. New York: McGraw-Hill.
Schurink, W.J. 1988. 'Designing Qualitative Research'. In *Research at Grassroots: A Primer for the Caring Professions*, edited by A.S. de Vos. Pretoria: J.L. van Schaik.
Searle, John R. 1969. *Speech Acts: An Essay in the Philosophy of Language*. Cambridge: Cambridge University Press.
Shabalala, Mbali. 1999. 'Homestead Names as a Reflection of Social Dynamics in Mabengela, Nkandla'. Master's thesis, University of Natal, Pietermaritzburg.
Shorter, Aylward. 1988. *Towards a Theology of Inculturation*. London: Geoffrey Chapman.
Smith, Edwin W. 1950. *African Ideas of God: A Symposium*. London: Edinburgh House.
Soga, John Henderson. 1931. *The Amaxosa: Life and Customs*. Alice: Lovedale Press.
Stewart, Julia. 1993. *African Names: Names from the African Continent for Children and Adults*. New York: Carol Publishing Group.
Strauss, John and Kalpana Mehra. 1990. 'Child Anthropometry in Côte d'Ivoire: Estimates from Two Surveys, 1985 and 1986'. *Journal of Public Economics* 61 (2): 155–92.
Strawson, Peter F. 1950. 'Mind'. *New Series* 59 (235): 320–44.
Stryker, Sheldon. 1980. *Symbolic Interactionism: A Social Structural Version*. Menlo Park, CA: Benjamin Cummings.
Suzman, Susan M. 1994. 'Names as Pointers: Zulu Personal Naming Practices'. *Language in Society* 23 (2): 253–72.
———. 2002. 'Zulu Names and Family Histories'. *Nomina Africana* 16 (1&2): 100–17.
Tabi, M.M., C. Doster and T. Cheney. 2010. 'A Qualitative Study of Women in Polygynous Marriages'. *International Nursing Review* 57 (1): 121–7.
Tempels, Placide. 1959. *Bantu Philosophy*. Paris: Collection Presence Africaine.
Ter Haar, Gerrie, ed. 2007. *Imagining Evil: Witchcraft Beliefs and Accusations in Contemporary Africa*. Trenton, NJ: Africa World Press.
Tertilt, Michèle. 2005. 'Polygyny, Fertility, and Savings'. *Journal of Political Economy* 113 (6): 1341–70.
Thipa, H.M. 1983. 'By Their Names You Shall Know Them'. *Names* 1 (2): 286–91.
Thobejane, Tsoaledi Daniel. 2014. 'An Exploration of Polygamous Marriages: A Worldview'. *Mediterranean Journal of Social Sciences* 5 (27): 1058–66.
Thorpe, S.A. 1991. *African Traditional Religions: An Introduction*. Pretoria: Unisa Press.
Triebel, Johannes. 2002. 'Living Together with the Ancestors: Ancestor Veneration in Africa as a Challenge for Missiology'. *Missiology* 30 (2): 187–97.
Trobisch, Walter. 1971. *My Wife Made me a Polygamist*. Illinois: Intervarsity Press.

Turner, Noleen. 1992. 'Zulu Names as Echoes of Censure, Discontent and Disapproval within the Domestic Environment'. *Nomina Africana* 6 (2): 42–56.

———. 1994. 'The Composition and Performance of Cryptic Social Messages in Zulu Onomastics'. *Voices: A Journal of Oral Studies* 1: 236–51.

———. 2003. 'Oral Strategies for Conflict Expression and Articulation of Criticism in Zulu Social Discourse'. PhD diss., University of Durban-Westville, Durban.

Uka, Emele Mba, ed. 1991. *Readings in African Traditional Religion: Structure, Meaning, Relevance, Future.* New York: Peter Lang.

Van Langendonck, Willy. 1983. 'Socio-Onomastic Properties of Bynames'. In *G.S. Nienaber: 'n Huldeblyk*, edited by A.J.L. Sinclair, 136–44. Bellville: University of the Western Cape Press.

———. 1987. 'Word Grammar and Child Grammar'. In *Belgian Journal of Linguistics: Perspectives on Child Language* 2 (1): 109–32.

———. 1990. 'Proper Names and Pronouns'. *Nomina Africana* 3 (1): 1–12.

———. 2001. 'Bynames within the Personal Name System'. *Nomina Africana* 15 (1&2): 203–11.

Van Rheenen, G. 1991. *Communicating Christ in Animistic Contexts.* Pasedena: William Carey Library.

Wagner, Natascha and Matthias Rieger. 2011. *Polygyny and Child Health: Do Babies Get Sick if Daddy Has Many Wives?* Geneva: Graduate Institute of International and Development Studies.

Wallace, Ruth A., ed. 1991. *Feminism and Sociological Theory.* Newbury Park, CA: Sage Publications.

West, Robert Cooper. 1976. *An Atlas of Louisiana Surnames of French and Spanish Origin.* Baton Rouge: Geoscience Publication

White, Clovis L. and Peter J. Burke. 1987. 'Ethnic Role Identity among Black and White College Students: An Interactionist Approach'. *Sociological Perspectives* 30 (3): 310–31.

Whorf, Benjamin L. 1956. 'An American Indian Model of the Universe'. In *Language, Thought and Reality: Selected Writings of Benjamin Lee Whorf*, edited by John. B. Carroll, 57–64. Cambridge, MA: MIT Press.

Wieschhoff, Heinrich Albert. 1941. *Colonial Policies in Africa.* Philadelphia: University of Pennsylvania Press.

Xulu, Muntu. 1987. *Kunje-ke!* Pietermaritzburg: Shuter & Shooter.

Zeitzen, Miriam Koktvedgaard. 2008. *Polygamy: A Cross-Cultural Analysis.* New York: Berg.

Zondi, Nompumelelo. 2012. 'Gender Inequality as a Recurring Theme in Songs Performed at a Specific Traditional and Ritual Ceremony in Zwelibomvu'. *Indilinga Journal of Indigenous Knowledge Systems* 11 (2): 194–205.

General Index

EBZ is Evangeline Bonisiwe Zungu.

acculturation 4–5, 17
Africa
    conflict in communal societies 18
    moral philosophy 76–7, 79–80
    religion 22–3, 32, 65, 82–3
African Renaissance 83
Africanism 140
Akan people (West Africa) 75, 126, 132
allusive language *see* language, allusive
ancestors *see* living-dead
anthroponymy *see* names, personal

Baluba (Congo) 77
birth 36–7, 98, 99; *see also* polygyny, and children
burial 73–4

ceremonies
cleansing 30–1, 75, 98
coming of age (*umemulo*) 30
chiefs 31
Christianity 5, 10
clothing 28, 29
community 137
Côte d'Ivoire 51
culture 3, 4, 17

death 20, 30–1, 74, 75–6, 77, 124, 129–30, 137; *see also* living-dead
defamation 140
divorce 13, 50

amadlozi see living-dead
dreams 23, 69
dress *see* clothing

ethnography 38, 39–41
extended families 13, 47

feminism 8, 54; *see also* women, and rights
fieldwork 39
food and drink 29–30, 31, 63–4

gender
    and power 46–8, 52–6; *see also* patriarchy
    as social construct 49
    and witchcraft 66
gerontocracy 46, 54
Ghana 47, 50
group identity 81–4
guilt 104

Haya community (Tanzania) 103
head taxes (*imali yekhanda*) 50
hegemonic masculinity *see* gender, and power
HIV/AIDS 6–7, 13, 45, 57
ukuhlonipha terms 43, 106

Ibibio people (Nigeria) 129
illness 70, 71

Khanyile, Jabu 139
ukukhuleka (shouting of praise names) 31
Khumalo, Leleti 139
Kranskop 27
KwaMambulu
  conflict in 123
  description of 2, 27–8
  dog names 100
  farming 50
  levirate marriage (*ukungena*) 45
  personal names 89–90, 98–9, 109–12, 113–14, 115–22, 129, 138, 145, 147–56
  poverty 51
  religion 27, 28, 138, 140
  research in 37–8, 43, 128
  social customs 28–37, 63–4, 138–9, 144–5
  witchcraft 66
  women of 27, 28–9, 32–3, 34–6, 45, 50, 51, 66

language 3–4, 14, 17, 100–1
  allusive 102, 107
life histories 42
living-dead (*amadlozi*) 19–20, 29, 30, 68–73, 74–8, 79, 82–3, 99, 104, 122, 126, 127, 129, 133, 137, 144–5
ilobolo (marriage negotiation) 9, 30, 32–3, 34, 50, 51, 93, 138–9, 141

Mabengela (Nkandla) 100
umabo (wedding gifts) 139
MaCele (fictional character) 60–1
MaKhumalo (fictional character) 61
MaNgwabe (fictional character) 61–2
marriage
  group 5

levirate (*ukungena*) 10, 34, 45, 58
negotiation *see ilobolo*
  as an oppressive institution 8, 50
  sororate (*ukuvus' amabele*) 35, 46
  Zulu custom 30, 31, 32–4, 35–6, 37, 51
  see also monogamy; polyandry; polygamy; polygyny
MaYeni (fictional character) 61
MaZondi (*isangoma*) 71–2
Mbeki, Thabo 83
menstruation 30, 47
misfortune 70, 71, 72, 78
umaMlambo (magical love potion) 112
monogamy 5, 7, 8, 9–10, 28–9, 139
Mormons 57–9
Mphakamiseni (fictional character) 78–9
Mseleku, Musa (fictional character) 59–60, 62
umuthi (traditional medicine) 21, 30, 108, 127, 128, 135

names
  African 18–19, 21, 22, 80, 84, 85–8, 143–4, 145–6
  allusive 102–3, 107
  Bhaca 126
  of dogs 100
  Euro-Western (*igama lesilungu*) 84–5, 92, 106, 141–3, 145–6
  given (patronyms) 107
  homestead 100
  and language 14
  of married women 60
  meaning and individual identity 81–2, 83, 84, 90–101, 128
  Nigeria 17, 86–7, 130–1
  parents' (teknonyms) 106–7
  Pedi 88

personal 15–16
proverbial 107–8
Shona 16–17
Sotho 96
South Africa 17
survival (penthonyms) 20, 124–7, 130–6
Uganda 88–9, 113
Venda 96
Xhosa 80, 96, 98
Zimbabwe 17
Zulu 1, 2, 5, 10, 16, 17–18, 20–1, 22, 23, 24–5, 88, 89–90, 91, 92, 93–4, 95, 96, 97, 98–9, 102–3, 104–8, 109–12, 113–14, 115–23, 124–6, 127, 128, 129, 131, 132–5, 140–1, 142–3, 145, 147–56
see also nicknames; surnames; specific forenames in Index of Personal Names
Nazareth Baptist Church (*abakwaShembe*) 28, 138, 140
izinduna 31
necromancy 68
Ngema, Mbongeni 139
Ngidi, Dumisani Mthandeni (EBZ's uncle) 1
Ngidi, Fikisiwe Thembeni (EBZ's grandmother) 1
Ngidi, Hloshana (EBZ's great-grandfather) 1–2
Ngidi, Jabulile Thembekile (EBZ's mother) 1
Ngidi, Mandoni (EBZ's great-grandmother) 1–2
Ngidi, Mphenyi (EBZ's grandfather) 1
izangoma (diviners) 19, 65, 66, 70–3, 113
nicknames 34, 102, 135

Niitsitapi (Blackfoot Indians, Canada) 16
nominal reincarnation 11–12
izinyanga (herbalists) 19, 65, 66, 70, 71

onomastics 15

Pandavas (Mahabharata, India) 6
participant observation 41
patriarchy 7–8, 9, 13, 24, 37, 44, 48, 52, 54, 56, 63
patronyms *see* names, given
penthonyms *see* names, survival
iphoyisa lenkosi (chief's police officer) 31
polyandry 5, 6, 8
polygamy 5
polygynists 9
polygyny
    adultery and divorce 7, 11, 13, 44
    and birth control 10
    and children 12–13, 45, 46, 50, 51, 52, 64, 138
    and Christianity 49
    and colonial administration 49–50
    and conflict 24, 36, 61, 94, 99, 103, 104, 108–23, 124, 140, 145
    definition of 5
    in fiction 57–63
    and HIV/AIDS 6–7, 13, 57
    and inheritance 115–16
    and Islam 8, 111
    and men 9, 10, 11, 12–13, 28–9, 44, 46, 47, 50, 55–7, 60, 62, 138, 139
    and Mormons 57–9
    and rural economy 12, 45, 50, 63–4
    urban 50
    and women 2, 7–8, 9, 11, 12, 13, 21, 24, 32, 35–6, 37, 44–5, 46, 47–9, 51–2, 54, 56–7, 60, 62–3, 72–3, 138, 139

praise songs (*izibongo*) 103

sacrifice 71, 72
Sapir-Whorf hypothesis 3–4
shame 10, 11, 18, 104
Shembe, Isaiah 138
'Sighs' (poem, Birago Diop) 73–4
Sister Wives (film) 59
songs and poetry 103–4
sons 36, 37, 138
sorcery *see* witchcraft
souls 23, 70, 73–4, 75
surnames 82, 106, 140

teknonyms *see* names, parents'
uThando NeS'thembu (film) 59–63

Three Wives, One Husband (film) 57–8
Tibet 6
Toda tribe (India) 6

ubuntu 83
Ulaka lwabaNguni (*The Wrath of the Nguni People*, I.S. Kubheka) 78–9

virginity testing 57

witchcraft (*ubuthakathi*) 23–4, 64–7, 70, 80, 112–13, 124, 127–9, 135
women
   barren 11, 36, 66
   and rights 8, 54, 57
words 14, 43, 86

Index of Personal Names

Alwande 150
Andile 150
Anele 90, 147
Aphelele 10, 147
Aphiwe 90
Asanda 150
Ayanda 150
Azande 150

Bachazani 110
Bafunani 151
Bagcinile 143
Bahlekabonke 111
Bajabhile 90, 103, 112
Bancamile 112, 125
Bandile 150
Banele 147
Bangifa 116
Bangifunani 108
Bantubazothini 151
Baphiwe 90
Baqhenyile 90
Bashongani 151
Bathini 22
Batwana 135
Bazothini 119, 151
Bhekamabomvu 90
Bhekamafa 1, 115
Bhekamuphi 114, 153
Bhekephi 153

Bhekimthetho 120
Bhekokwakhe 154
Bhekubala 109
Bhekumuthi 23, 103, 129
Bizwephi 153
Bonabeganwa 93
Bonani 151
Bongangani 134, 151
Bongathini 116, 134, 151
Bonisiwe 85
Buhlebethu 89
Bukani 99, 151
Bulewephi 113–14, 153
Busangokwakhe 154
Buselaphi 153
Buyelaphi 113, 153
Buyenzeni 151
Buzakunyoko 1, 117
Buzaliphi 153
Buzelukwenzani 107

Cabangeni 151
Cebani 151
Cebolenkosi 89
Celani 151
Chotsani 127

Dingilizwe 126
Dlezakhe 116
Duduzile 90

173

Dumazigugu 104–5
Dumeleni 151

Falakhe 154
Falinzima 126
Felamandla 23, 129
Fihlokwakhe 154
Fihlwaphi 94, 153
Fikanaye 119
Fikelephi 21, 114, 153
Fikenani 151
Fisani 151
Fisukwenzani 151
Fumbetheni 23, 121, 129
Funani 151
Fundakubona 120
Fundakwezakhe 154
Fungeleni 151
Funokwakhe 154

Gadla 131
Gcinabazali 98
Gcinangokubusa 115
Gcinetheni 151
Gcinokwakhe 116, 154
Gigigi 97
Ginsiginsi 135
Gqibokwakhe 115–16, 154
Gwazakwenkunzi 135

Hambephi 153
Hlabangane 90
Hlalaleni 151
Hlalempini 120, 151
Hlalephi 153
Hlalezwini 98
Hlalisile 98
Hlanganani 151
Hlanyukiwe 109

Hlebani 94, 151
Hlengiwe 92
Hletshiwe 108
Hleziphi 153
Hlokomani 151
Hlomesakhe 154
Hlulwayini 151
Hlushwayini 21, 110, 151

Jabulile 106
Jaheni 151

Khalani 151
Khalathi 150
Khalazome 95
Khangwayini 151
Khanyisani 151
Khawulani 114, 152
Khethowakhe 154
Khohlwangifile 122
Khohlwayezakhe 111, 154
Khokhaziphi 153
Kholwangani 152
Khonangani 152
Khonani 152
Khongaphi 154
Khonjwenzeni 152
Khonzangani 152
Khonzaphi 154
Khonzeni 152
Khula 134
Khulelaphi 113, 154
Khulumani 152
Khumbula 92
Khwezi 125
Kwanda 150
Kwanele 10, 90
Kwazikwakhe 155
Kwenzakufani 152

Index of Personal Names

Kwenzakuni 152
Kwenzakuyashiyana 135
Kwenzakwakhe 155
Kwenzeleni 152

Langalibalele 125
Lindeni 152
Lindiwe 92
Lufuno 96
Lungeleni 152
Luyanda 150
Lwazi 89

Mabhunu 150
Madodanenzani 135
Mafungwase 125
Magamakhe 94
Mahlomeka 107
Maqinsiqinsi 135
Mathufela 97
Mawande 150
Mazubale 126
Mbangiseni 115, 147
Mbhasobheni 134, 147
Mbhekeni 147
Mbizwa 147
Mboneni 147
Mbongwa 147
Mbukelwa 147
Mbukeni 147
Mbulaleni 133, 147
Mbusiseni 147
Mbuyiselwa 147
Mbuyiseni 132, 147
Mbuzeni 135, 147
Mcabangiseni 147
Mcanukelwa 147
Mcebiseni 147
Mchazeleni 132, 147

Mchitheni 131, 148
Mcingeni 134, 148
Mdindeni 108, 148
Mdingi 148
Mdubane 150
Mduduzi 90
Mdumazeni 133, 148
Mdumiseni 140
Melwawubani 121, 152
Mfana 135
Mfanafuthi 89, 125
Mfaniseni 148
Mfihlelwa 148
Mfihleni 133
Mfiselwa 148
Mfulathelwa 148
Mfungelwa 148
Mgababa 150
Mgabiselwa 148
Mganiseni 148
Mgezeni 148
Mhlabunzima 148
Mhlaliseni 133, 148
Mhlalisi 148
Mhlekude 148
Mhlekwa 148
Mhlengeni 132, 148
Mhletshwa 110, 148
Mhlonipheni 148
Mhlonishwa 148
Minenhle 125
Mkakeni 148
Mkhanyiseni 148
Mkhanyisi 148
Mkhetheni 133, 148
Mkhethwa 148
Mkhipheni 93
Mkhohliseni 131, 148
Mkhombiseni 148

Mkhonzeni 148
Mkhululeni 132, 148
Mkhulunyelwa 148
Mlahleni 96, 148
Mlandeni 133, 148
Mlindwa 148
Mlungeleni 134, 148
Mmiseni 133, 149
Mnikelo 98
Mnikeni 133, 149
Mnikwa 149
Mntukatshelwa 149
Mnukwa 149
Mosa 126
Moyomusha 106, 120
Mpemeawu 107–8
Mphakamiseni 78–9, 149
Mphenduleli 149
Mphenyi 149
Mphindeni 149
Mphiwa 149
Mphumuzeni 132, 149
Mpisendlini 125
Mqabuli 97
Mqiniseni 132, 149
Mqondisi 149
Mshangane 150
Mshin'ozishintshayo 107
Mthandeni 133, 149
Mthembeni 149
Mthethokayizwani 94, 120, 149
Mthinteni 134
Mthobeleni 149
Mthokozeleni 149
Mtholeni 149
Mtholephi 149
Mtsheleni 149
Mtshengiseni 133, 149
Mtuseni 149

Mudemude 107
Muntukabani 119
Muziwenduku 120
Mvikeleni 127, 133, 149
Mvuseni 149
Mxoleleni 132, 149
Myekeni 127, 132, 149
Mzameleni 149
Mzamiseni 149
Mzibeni 96, 149
Mzikabani 155
Mzikawubongwa 155
Mzikawukhalelwa 155
Mzikayifani 152, 155
Mzikayise 155
Mzileni 149
Mziweqili 155
Mzobanzi 155
Mzokhanyayo 155
Mzokhethiwe 155
Mzokhona 155
Mzokhulayo 155
Mzomuhle 155
Mzondeni 96, 133, 149
Mzonjani 155
Mzonzima 113, 149, 155
Mzothulayo 155
Mzovukayo 155
Mzumeni 149
Mzungezeni 114, 132, 149
Mzuvele 155
Mzwakhe 155
Mzwamandla 155
Mzwandile 156
Mzwangedwa 117
Mzwempi 156
Mzwendoda 156
Mzwenduna 156
Mzwenhlanhla 156

Mzwenkosi 156
Mzwethu 156
Mzwoxolo 156

Nakowubani 152
Nakwawubani 118
Ncengani 152
Ncengutshwala 110
Ndabiyesinda 110
Nduduzo 90
Ngenzeleni 116, 152
Nginakenani 99
Nginikabani 143
Nginikani 152
Ngizomphani 117, 152
Ngoneni 118, 152
Ngwanenyana 126
Nhlalayenza 122
Nhlanhla 89, 140
Nkabenkulu 97
Nkalakatha 97
Nkosiyangithanda 20
Nkosiyombango 115
Nobelungu 150
Nobesuthu 150
Nobuhle 95, 96
Nobusuku 125
Nokubonga 89
Nokudinga 125
Nokusa 125
Nokwazi 89
Nokwethemba 89
Noluthando 89
Nomabhayi 151
Nomabhomu 150
Nomachweba 151
Nomadlozi 125
Nomagoli 151
Nomakhimbili 151

Nomakula 150
Nomangisi 150
Nomasonto 90, 125
Nomaswazi 150
Nombeko 96
Nomfundo 22, 89, 95, 96
Nomgqibelo 90, 125
Nomkhosi 143
Nomkhuleko 125
Nomkhumbi 89
Nompumelelo 95, 96
Nomsebenzi 98
Nonjabulo 89
Nonkantolo 125
Nontobeko 92
Nozipho 92
Nqubeko 90
Nsizwa 125
Nsukukazifani 152
Ntandoni 121, 152
Ntandoyeningi 89
Ntombazane 135
Ntombenjani 152
Ntombi 125
Ntombifuthi 89
Ntombintathu 89, 125
Ntombizaphi 117, 154
Ntokozo 89
Nyathelephi 23, 114, 129, 154

Phakamani 152
Phathokwakhe 155
Phelelani 147
Phendulani 152
Phephelaphi 154
Phethelaphi 154
Philangani 152
Philangenkosi 131
Philangomusa 20

Philasande 134, 150
Philile 98
Phiweni 152
Phothani 152
Phumasilwe 120
Phumowakhe 155
Puleng 96

Qamndile 99
Qapheleni 119, 152
Qedusizi 98
Qhamukephi 119, 154
Qhoshangani 152
Qinisela 16
Qondeni 152
Qondokwakhe 155

Sabani 152
Sakhamuphi 154
Sakhephi 154
Sakhiseni 152
Sandile 150
Sandiso 150
Sanele 90, 147
Sbusiso 106
Sebenzeyakhe 155
Senzeni 152
Sethembene 89
Setheni 152
Shiyaliphi 154
Shokwakhe 155
Sholiphi 22, 154
Shongani 153
Shongaziphi 143, 154
Sibahlesonke 89
Sibangaliphi 118, 154
Sibangani 153
Sibani 98
Sibongiseni 89

Sibusisiwe 140
Sibusiso 140
Sibuyiselwe 20
Sihlezinenkosi 96
Simethembeni 121, 153
Simosakhe 155
Simphiwe 90
Singaphi 154
Sinqobile 92
Sipho 16, 106
Sisanda 150
Siyanda 150
Siyathokoza 125
Sizophila 131
Sizwayini 153
Skhandamayeza 135
Skhumbuzo 92
Slondiwe 92
Smangele 92
Solani 153
Songeleni 153
Sonosakhe 95, 155
Sphelele 147
Sphelelisiwe 147
Sphephelo 108
Sweleni 153

Thandanani 89
Thandekile 98
Thandephi 154
Thandonjani 153
Thandowakhe 155
Thandwangubani 109
Thangithini 94, 110, 153
Thathezakhe 155
Thathokwakhe 155
Thembekile 89
Thembelenkosini 89
Thembeni 153

Thembokwakhe 121, 155
Thokozaphi 154
Thuleleni 153
Thuthukani 90
Tshelwawubani 153
Tshenwephi 111, 154
Tshovo 135

Usanda 150

Velemseni 89
Velephi 154
Veluyeke 118
Vimbephi 112, 154
Vuloyi 106
Vumeleni 153

Wandile 150

Yekezakhe 20

Zamahlomuka 90
Zamokwakhe 155
Zamukwanda 150

Zamukwenzani 153
Zandile 150
Zanele 147
Zehlile 90
Zibelani 117, 153
Zibeleni 25, 103
Zibizendlela 131
Zibokwakhe 155
Zibuyile 90
Zimbili 89
Zithathephi 154
Ziyanda 150
Zizile 92
Zobephi 154
Zodlani 153
Zokwenzani 118, 121, 153
Zondani 109
Zophiwani 125
Zothephi 154
Zotholani 114, 153
Zuzani 153
Zwabethini 153
Zwelinjani 103
Zweni 153

Printed and bound by CPI Group (UK) Ltd, Croydon, CR0 4YY
06/04/2026

14854581-0003